LOVE
Lifted
ME

BOBBY DENTON

HERITAGE BUILDERS
PUBLISHING

ABOUT THE AUTHOR

Former Alabama State Senator Bobby Denton and his wife Barbara have been married 58 years. They have three children, three grandchildren, and two great-grandchildren.

Senator Denton began a successful career in music at a young age, appeared on national television in 1958, and was inducted into the Alabama Music Hall of Fame in 2010. He has recorded 87 songs and written three books during his lifetime, and performs live as a hobby.

The senator retired from the State Senate in 2010 after serving eight consecutive terms for a total of 32 years, and was the Dean of the Senate. He is the longest continually serving State Senator in the history of Alabama.

He is retired from Ford Motor Company and Northwest-Shoals Community College, and is a former business owner and bank executive.

He is a member of the Church of Christ, a graduate of Cherokee Vocational High School, and the University of Alabama.

HERITAGE BUILDERS PUBLISHING
© 2015

Contributing Editor, Mason Smith
Book and Cover Design, Eliasson Marketing
Published by Heritage Builders Publishing
Clovis, Montery California 93619

www.heritagebuilders.com   1-888-898-9563

ISBN 978-1-942603-07-8

Printed and bound in the United States of America

CHAPTER ONE

Love is patient and kind; love is not jealous or boastful; it is not arrogant or rude; love does not insist on its own way; it is not enviable or resentful; it does not rejoice at wrong, but rejoices in the right; love bears all things; believes all things; hopes all things; and endures all things. (I Corinthians 13:4-7).

The scriptures say that God even knew us while we were still in our mother's womb. It is hard to comprehend the power of God and His love for us. He can see the future and even knows the intentions of our hearts.

Saturday, August 13th, 1938, was a hot and steamy summer day. In the late afternoon, the pains of childbirth could be heard all around the little house on a rocky hillside seven miles south of Cherokee, Alabama, on White Pike Road near the Alabama-Mississippi state line. As the labor pains grew more intense, the children were all sent walking down the gravel road to the house of an aunt and uncle about a half-mile away. The four children could still hear the groans and chilling cries of their mother as she was giving birth. They were afraid and could only hope that it was going to be all right. The oldest child, 13-year old Vera, held the hand of her 5-year old sister Dorothy as the boys, Buddy age 10, and Johnny, 7, walked down the road away from the house where the baby was being born.

At 6:00 p.m., Lillie Mae Denton, who was 34-years old, gave birth to the sixth child she had given birth to with her husband, 39-year old Dewey Denton. Their first child, a baby girl, was stillborn on January 3rd, 1924. With the kind help of two close friends and Dr. Finley, the old doctor who practiced medicine in Cherokee, a healthy baby boy was born. They named him Bobby Eugene.

It is said that only God's love for us exceeds a mother's love. Only after we get older do we begin to really appreciate her love and all the things she did for us. We will never know the extent of her loving care and the sacrifices she endured to give birth and raise us.

I can't recall the first thing that I remember after my birth, but I know it was at an early age. A few of the events had to occur when I was less than two years old. I believe the first was sitting on my granddaddy Denton's lap at his and granny's house, which was only about 100 yards from where we lived. I was just a baby because I was only two years old when he died. I had been sick and my mother carried me, wrapped in a blanket, to his house to see his body in the casket. Also, I remember as just a toddler walking down the path to my grandparents' house with my daddy. I held on to his finger as we walked, and it made me feel safe and loved.

For the next several years, only flashbacks come to my mind of tiny episodes of family and the day-to-day things. I do remember in World War II the restrictions on buying some goods like sugar, baking flour, coffee, tea, tires and other things. It seemed that I was really somebody as a child to have government stamps in my own name. Of course, that's the way they distributed the rationing stamps to buy these short supply commodities during the war. Every family member was allotted stamps to present to the store when the items were purchased. These were the only things we really needed because we raised almost everything else except our clothing, and a lot of those were made of material the flour was bagged in. My mother made her or my older sisters a dress when she had saved several flour bags. Most of the cloth bags had small designs on them and were two colors, like a white background with blue flowers.

Although my parents rarely attended church, they had high family values. They taught us the basic good things like helping and respecting others, especially older people. We never worked on Sundays and were taught to love God and keep his commandments. In those days parents loved their children differently than we do today. They gave the kids space and didn't hover over them every minute. As long as the parents knew where their children were, they let them play and imagine and create things for themselves. It was deep love, but a tougher love. I know my mother and daddy would have killed or died for me if it were necessary; however, they never used the spoken word for love, they never spoke the words "I love you." They never did at all, but I know they did. The unspoken love they gave me was even more powerful. I never gave it a thought as to whether my parents loved me or not. I knew they did, so that was all that mattered.

Discipline is a very important form of love. I can remember only a very few times I received what we now call a spanking. They were called whippings back then. The whippings that I received were always with love, never once abusive. I do not remember verbal abuse being used towards me or my siblings. We all were raised to respect our parents and our parents respected us. However, there are times that a good whipping was just what the child needed. Children who receive discipline with love will love their parents more and become a better person. The Holy Scripture even says "spare the rod and spoil the child." (Proverbs 13:24)

I remember as a young boy growing up far out in the country during the 1940's, we mostly spent our Sundays resting or visiting family and friends. Everyone had a fresh bath and clean clothes for the day. I don't remember going to Church for a regular worship service. However, every summer we attended two or three Churches for what was called all-day singing and dinner-on-the-ground events.

These were special days for kids. We never went inside the building to hear the singing. That was for the older people. The kids roamed the area and played all day, except for when the long tables outside the Church were filled with all kinds of good food. Back then, the kids had to eat last after all the grown-ups had filled their plates.

Then after dinner, the older people went back inside and sang all afternoon. You could hear them singing from a mile away. The

Church buildings where the singings were held had a big upright piano and there werc always several master players who could bang out all those old gospel songs with vigor. Just about all the piano players were nicely dressed ladies who loved every minute of the attention they were getting while playing for the crowd.

I remember going to a Gospel meeting which was called a "revival" back then at the Mt. Zion Church, located a few miles from where we lived. It was exciting getting to go somewhere as a kid after it was dark outside. They had oil lamps mounted on the walls of the little church for light. For me, the best part about going to the meeting was the music. An out-of-the area preacher and his wife sang and played the guitar and accordion. I had never seen an accordion before. It had a keyboard like a piano, but it also had small buttons on it. The player had it strapped over his shoulders and it rested at his chest where he squeezed it from side-to-side with his hands making the sound.

They mostly played up-tempo, foot-patting Gospel songs and the little church rocked with appreciation and praise to the Lord. After entertaining the crowd for a while, the preacher would give a fiery sermon for about an hour.

For a small boy living out in the country with no form of enter-tainment other than a battery powered radio at home, this was a special event. And the radio was only allowed until my parents went to bed early at night.

Although music has been my passion all my life, I never sang Gospel music while I was growing up. However, since I began recording again in 1996, I have recorded dozens of Gospel Songs.

A lot of time in my early years was spent playing with my cousins Betty Sue and Linda Williams. They lived just down the road from my house. We would play "make believe" stuff which most of the time turned out to be playing "play house". Me being the boy, I was always the head of the house, or the husband and father. Later, two boys who were grandsons of Mrs. Hamilton, who lived about two miles away, moved back from out west with their parents. Bobby and Baxter Bozeman were a welcome addi-tion to my life. They were about my age and we seemed to develop deep friendships from the beginning. The boys and I spent all our spare time doing things together. Their early years were developed under better economic conditions than mine; however, I was more grounded in the area of work on the farm and chores around the house. The Bozeman boys and I built a cabin in the woods, swam in the creek, and pretended to be about anyone we could imagine. There were three other boys who played a role in my early childhood. They were the twins, Marvin and Garvin Daily, and Nathan Wallace. They did not live in the immediate community but we had opportunities to spend time together and continued our friendship through high school. The imagination is a great teacher in developing children. Without TV and modern-day toys, the children used the power of imagination in their play and it helped them to learn.

I always had a passion regarding radio towers and antennas. As a small boy, before we got electricity, I would string a little copper wire from our battery operated radio to a tree outside a window and receive a clear signal from the radio stations. One time, when I was very young, we went to visit relatives in Florence and I saw a radio station tower. It amazed me, and I wondered how it was built and how it worked. Playing radio station then became my latest imaginary toy. Never did I dream that building towers for radio stations and TV antennas would be my business for several years when I was in my thirties. Life was hard for the family when I was a young boy but we didn't know it because most everyone we knew was like us. Sometimes, we found ourselves feeling sorry for a few families because they didn't have the things we had.

My daddy worked at the Reynolds Aluminum Plant in Muscle Shoals for a few years after World War II as we continued to maintain a small farming operation along with having the usual vegetable gardens, a cow, pigs and chickens. We also had two excellent mules, Belle and Ella, that were used for the farming work. We also had what we called a plug mule named Mandy. A spare mule, or plug mule like Mandy, was used for single plowing and other purposes around the farm. We raised cotton and corn. The cotton was sold and the corn was used to feed the animals. We also took shelled corn to town and had it ground into cornmeal for bread. We worked hard in the fields; however, my older brothers did most of the work.

My granddaddy, John Amos Denton, who died when I was 2-years old, owned a very large tract of land. But, when he died, we only had the few acres for our home facilities. The remaining land was purchased by other family members and we didn't have good land to farm. So we farmed a tract of land a few miles down the road. I remember picking cotton and doing all the other farm work that had to be done. As a kid, I wondered why we were giving Mrs. Hamilton some of our cotton and corn. Never had I heard the term "share cropper". That's what we did with the little farm. We used Mrs. Hamilton's land and gave her a share of the crop that was produced.

One of the most exciting times in my life was getting electricity. Riding the school bus home every day I could see the progress of the construction for the power lines. There were no power tools and all the holes for the power line poles were dug by hand with hole diggers. It was very time-consuming. Day after day I would see the progress of getting the power lines to our house. In anticipation of having electric power for our house, my daddy and a cousin wired the house and installed the things necessary to use electric power.

One has to experience what it is like living without electricity to fully appreciate having it. There is no bright lighting, no refrigerator, ice, hot water, cooking stove, and all the things that we take for granted as we use them every day. Days and weeks passed as I looked through the window of the school bus anticipating the day when the power was turned on. It was an absolutely incredible feeling the day that I got off the school bus and ran into the house, turning on lights which were placed in the center of the ceiling in every room. The light was bright! I can't remember the size of the bulbs, but they were 60 or 100 watts, I suppose. But after using an oil lamp in the room all my life, it was fabulous.

Over the next year, our life changed a lot. The first thing was a new refrigerator, then a clothes washing machine, a new electric radio, a new cooking stove and an electric iron. My mother was so happy to get these wonderful appliances after working so hard without them all her life. By this time, my older sister, Vera, had married Earl (Quinn) Lair of Cherokee and my older brother, Buddy, was out of high school and was married to Lorene Hunt of Sheffield. Johnny soon followed them, dropping out of school and marrying very young. My sister Dorothy did the same within two years.

By this time, the farming was over and only my mother and daddy and I were still there in the little house.

CHAPTER TWO

A turn in my life occurred when I was about nine years old. From a young man, my daddy had been musically inclined and could play a five-string banjo very well. I remember his talking about him and a friend, Leonard McCaig, riding mules for long distances when they were young men to play music for square dances. He also was a champion buck dancer and could still dance quite well until he reached 90 years of age. He won blue ribbons for several years at the Helen Keller Festival in Tuscumbia. As he became older, we often thought that the excessive exercise might be bad for him, but I suppose it proved to be good therapy; he lived to be 92. Daddy could play almost any instrument, but the banjo was his choice.

For some reason a lady who lived a few miles away asked if she could borrow his banjo to try to play it. In return she would let him keep an old guitar that she had. With the love for music already in my system, I began trying to play that old guitar. My daddy knew a few simple chords and taught them to me. I would strum and sing songs every day when I came home from school. After a few months, the lady's son brought the banjo back to us and was to pick up the guitar. I would have done anything to keep the instrument but I had no say in the matter. The lady's son who came to my house to get the guitar was sweethearts with my cousin Christine Williams. He evidently wanted to impress her with his temper. They had a brief argument on the front porch as they were leaving our house. Holding the guitar by its neck like one would hold a baseball bat, he swung it hard striking a post on the front porch, breaking the guitar into a thousand pieces. I could not believe it; he destroyed something I would love to have had. Now it was gone. To say the least, it was a bad thing he did and we didn't know what to do. There was nothing any of us could say. I was raised to forgive, but I could never forget what he had done.

After the music bug had bitten me, I became more interested in listening to songs on the radio and dreaming of someday becoming involved with music. Another distant cousin, Don Denton, had a guitar that his parents had ordered for him from Sears and Roebuck; the big mail order company that published a catalogue with just about everything in it. I saw the guitar at his house while we were visiting his family. It was a Silver Tone and looked just like new. I asked them about it and they said that Don never took any interest in playing it and I could use it for a while. I couldn't wait to get home with it to play. It had a cord that allowed me to stand up and play, so I would stand up playing and singing like a big star. One day while performing for my mother, standing in the living room, the cord holding the guitar broke and the instrument hit the hard floor.

At first, I thought it was going to be fine and that no damage was done; however, when I picked it up the back side was cracked from front to back. My next thought was that I was going to be in big trouble, but I was so glad my mother was there to see what happened. When my dad came home from work, I was terrified that he would be upset with me.

In my mind I thought, "I'm not having very much luck with using someone else's guitar." My dad was calm and said, "we'll just have to tell Don and his family what happened and try to find someone to fix it."

During the next few days we took the guitar over to my cousin's house in the Maude community about 10 miles away. I was so sorry that this had happened and didn't know what would be the outcome.

When we got to Riley and Lessie Denton's house I was shak-

15

ing in my shoes. I just knew they and their son Don would be mad at me, but when we showed them the crack in the guitar and told them what happened, Riley said, "Well that's alright, you can just have it."

My heart almost jumped out of my chest. Daddy later found someone to repair the crack with glue and I enjoyed playing it for a long time.

Whenever we visited relatives and friends in the community, I always carried my guitar and was the entertainment. That Silver Tone with the crack down its back was a treasure to me. I carried it to school on special days and would play and sing to the class if the teacher requested it.

In 1950 I was 12 years old and considered to be the last child my parents would have. However, on February 15th, 1950, my mother gave birth to a baby girl and they named her Cala Sue. My mother was 45 and my dad was 50. The family worried whether my parents would be able to care for her as they grew older. Cala was the best thing that ever happened to my parents. She was so sweet and smart and lovable. Everyone was happy that we had her in the family. In school she was a straight "A" student and a cheer-leader for the high school.

In the meantime, my little music career continued to develop and opportunities came along often. At the age of 14, I teamed up with two older boys who could play music extremely well. Bobby and Julian Henry lived several miles from me across what was called Freedom Hills. They had a car so they came to my house often to play music. Almost every session would include a tune or two from daddy on his banjo. As time went on another friend from the Rock Creek community, Bobby Rogers, joined with us play-ing the bass fiddle. When I was 15, our little group was playing on local radio stations in the Muscle Shoals area and had established ourselves as upcoming young entertainers.

Later, we were invited to come to Nashville to sing and play on the WSM radio program called The Junior Grand Ole Opry and compete for a guest spot on the real Grand Ole Opry, along with other prizes. When the big day came we all loaded up in the 1949

Ford car of Julian's and took off for Nashville before daybreak with stardom dancing in our heads. We did the radio program that Saturday along with a few other contestants and drove the long 150 miles back home. It was a big deal and a dream come true for me. Singing on one of the most popular and powerful radio stations in the country was breathtaking. We had to wait a week to learn who would advance to the final competition. With my ear glued to the radio the next Saturday, I could not believe it when the announcer called out "the winner is Bobby Denton from Cherokee, Alabama." This meant that the next week we would go back to Nashville to compete for the final prize. By this time the whole area of North-west Alabama was pulling for us to win the finals. The second trip to the Music City was even more exciting. We sang and played with confidence of winning. The next week was long, waiting for the results of who the winner would be. It was heartbreaking to learn that a girl from Kentucky was the top winner and we were runner-up. The group continued to perform around the area and playing on radio programs.

While we were at a radio station in Florence one Saturday to record 15 minute segments for the next week's early morning pro-grams, a young guy came into the studio and said, "I'm Kelso Her-ston. I just got home from the army and would like to play guitar with ya'll." In my mind I thought, "Well, we already have Julian playing the electric guitar and Bob playing the steel guitar, and there's me playing the acoustic guitar," but we all agreed that we should let him sit in with us for a few songs thinking he could just be a "wannabe" player. Wow, was Kelso a player. He had learned to play stuff in the army that we had never heard before. I had no idea that Kelso would later co-found the little recording company in Florence that asked me to record the first master record in Ala-bama. He later played on my records that were made in the famous Owen Bradley Studio in Nashville, and went on to be one of the top music producers in the country. The little band took on two new members over the next year, my beautiful older sister Dot, and a boy named O'Neal Bishop from Tuscumbia. Dot was a good singer, and O'Neal played the guitar and also could sing well. We were successful performing around the region. We entered the big talent show at the Mid-South Fair in Memphis and won first place, the blue ribbon. This gave me and the others popularity and opened many new doors for us in the future.

After discussing the possibility of moving from the little house where I was born, my parents made the decision to move to town. There seemed to be no reason to live in the house seven miles from town any more. The family was gone, building their own lives; my little sister Cala and I were the only kids remaining at home. We rented an older house in Cherokee and moved in. The house was not as modern as most, but it was better than our old house in the country. It really was a big change for us but we soon became accustomed to being closer to stores and the schools. It was nice to be able to walk to downtown in just a few minutes. One could buy almost everything for everyday use in the small town. It had a Post Office, Drug Store, Barber Shop, and three general merchandise stores. General merchandise stores were like a super small Wal-Mart, selling everything from groceries to clothing and hardware. For the larger variety of things the people would drive or ride a bus to what we called uptown, which was the Tri-cities of Tuscumbia, Sheffield, and Florence. Muscle Shoals was in place, but just beginning to develop from its incorporation in 1923.

Most of the land in Muscle Shoals was owned by out-of-state property speculators who believed that Henry Ford would go through with the purchase of the newly constructed Wilson Dam by President Roosevelt's new deal plan. The dam was a master-piece of modern construction and served as a flood control and river navigational system. Wilson Dam could also produce massive amounts of electricity at a very low cost. Henry Ford's plan was to purchase the dam for abundant electric power to his auto plant he was planning to build near Muscle Shoals. If the U.S. Congress had not blocked the sale of the dam to Ford, the huge auto plant at Detroit, Michigan, would have been built just east of Muscle Shoals. Still, today there are sidewalks, fire hydrants and other infrastructure in the City of Muscle Shoals that were put in place in anticipation of the Ford Motor Company development. Also, almost every street in Muscle Shoals has a sister street by the same name in Detroit.

After moving to town, I had a wider variety of new friends to associate with. I found that my interests began to change as I spent more time with friends and hanging out in town. My school work was of no interest to me, and every year I had to struggle to move to the next grade level. Two of my closest friends, Larry Daniel and Wheeler Benson, were excellent students, but I never thought that education would be anything that I would need. All I wanted to be was an entertainer some day. My time at home with my parents and little sister was just not exciting enough for me. We didn't have a television or phone, and there was not the incentive for my imagination to amuse myself as it was in the isolation of the country house.

As time went by, I began to venture out more and I spent most of my time going and doing things with friends. I also made a special friend through my association with music who lived in Florence. Tom Stafford was a few years older and worked at the Shoals Theater in Florence as assistant manager. Tom's dad owned and operated the City Drug Store just down the street from the movie house. Since I was only 15 and didn't have a car, most of the trips that I made to Florence on weekends to visit with Tom consisted of hitch-hiking a ride. I would stand out on the side of Highway 72 in Cherokee with my guitar and catch a ride. Everybody that didn't have a car did that in those days. I never dreamed of it being dangerous at all. Tom loved music and was a good short story and song writer. Although he was somewhat eccentric, he was a good person. He and I would collaborate on writing songs and dreamed of making good in the music business some day. Tom and I worked together well and were the catalyst for the later development of the famous recording studio upstairs over the City Drug Store which was the beginning point of several young musicians who later made it very big in music.

The downside of coming to Florence and working with Tom was all the time I spent waiting for him to get off work at the theater. But that waiting time became a blessing to me later. When

I came to Florence I spent nights at my older brother's house in Sheffield. Buddy had been drafted into the army and his wife Lorene and her mother, Mrs. Hunt, lived on 14th Avenue in Sheffield. Lorene was an accomplished beautician and owned a beauty salon. She was a great help to me as a young teen in those days.

Lorene and Buddy's house was located next door to a very nice couple who had two girls. The neighbors, Eugene and Myrtie Lee Jeffreys, were kind and loving people, and never met a person they didn't like. I had noticed the daughters, Barbara who was 13, and Carolyn 8, around the yard, and the family would always speak to me when I came to my brother's house. Barbara was a little reserved and Carolyn was a spirited and animated younger sister. When one is 15 years old we have a tendency to think of the person who is two years younger as too much of a kid to think beyond "Hi, how are you?" In school there were a couple of girls whom I would have liked to have been sweethearts with, but they never seemed to want me as a boyfriend. I had never been on a date and knew almost nothing about the "birds and bees". Barbara became prettier and nicer almost every time I would see her. God's plan for me was beginning to take shape in this new time of my life, but I didn't think in those terms then; I never thought much about spiritual matters.

CHAPTER THREE

After meeting Barbara several times, we became at ease talking with each other in the yard when I was at my brother's house. Her daddy and mother were so nice, and the little sister, Carolyn, was always there and talking more than Barbara. One weekend while I was waiting for Tom Stafford to get off work, I decided not to waste my time sitting in the movie so I went across the street to a Drug Store that had telephone booths and called Barbara's house. Back then the phones were not the dial type; you had to give the number you were calling to a live operator. I found an empty phone booth and picked up the receiver and inserted a dime to make the call.

The operator said "Number please," then I said "3456J, please." Luckily Barbara answered the phone. I was relieved that I didn't have to ask one of her parents if I could speak with her. She was nice to talk with and we enjoyed our conversations very much. Sometimes we would talk for a long time, and the calls to Barbara became an important part of my weekend visits to the Tri-Cities. I believe that her parents only allowed her to talk to me because they trusted me as their neighbor's brother. The phone calls continued for about a year, becoming longer and longer. At times we would sit on the front porch swinging and talking but very seldom in private because Carolyn was always around. She didn't want to miss a thing, and we would have loved for her to go inside the house and leave us alone. As the months went by, I remember sitting in my room at our house in Cherokee writing letters to Barbara. As I mentioned before, we didn't have a phone, so just writing a letter during the week would help me keep in touch with her, although most of the letters were never mailed.

Things remained about the same in school as I struggled every day of it. My music continued to be my main interest, along with always having a job around town. My daddy purchased a new power lawnmower to cut our grass at home and I used it to mow lawns all around town. People would pay me from $2.00 to $5.00 to cut their grass depending on the size of their yard. I always had a side job doing about anything that needed to be done. The money was used as my spending money for visits to the Drug Store soda fountain, and hanging out with my friends. Some of the best times that I had were delivering the Birmingham News paper all over town with Wheeler Benson on his motor scooter. He would drive and I would throw the rolled up papers. I don't know why, but everybody called Wheeler "Poodak". We all had nicknames; my nickname was "George" because of a joke I had told my friends about a rabbit. We never did anything really bad except smoke cigarettes when we could afford them. A pack of cigarettes cost 20 cents. I remember when they went up to 21 cents and a coke went up from a nickel to 6 cents. The drink companies installed a little box on the side of the machine to put the penny in.

The most fun thing we boys did was play football at Bobby Knight's house. They had a vacant lot next door and it made a perfect place to play. Several of these kids turned out to be star football players in high school. Along with Bobby Knight, there were Buddy Willis, Jack Cochran, Buster Borden, Kenneth Jones, Carter Reid, Howard Keeton, Larry Nelson and others. I have often bragged about being a part of the outstanding football program at Cherokee Vocational High School back in the 50's. I tell people that I played the position of dummy for the first team players. As the third string center, I didn't get a lot of playing time in most games, unless the score was a runaway in Cherokee's favor.

My oldest sister Vera and her husband Quinn lived in Chero-kee, and that was my second home. Quinn was my hero and taught me so much. He was smart and wise in a lot of things. My sister Vera loved me as if I was her own child and gave me money to go to the movie hundreds of times. They had not yet had their two children, George and Beth Susan, so I was like their little boy in my early years.

We had an old movie theater in Cherokee, and even got a drive-in movie in the 50's. I worked for my friend Alan Ray Ligon's dad when he built the new drive-in movie. The first regular theater was already in place when the Ligon family moved to Cherokee. Before Mr. Ligon bought and remodeled the old movie house, I remember that it didn't have the usual sloping floor toward the front. It had wood bench seats that got higher at each row toward the back, so if one sat in the back it was high off of the floor. I remember a Saturday, while watching a Western movie, one of the kids became so excited about a bad cowboy beating up on a good guy that he threw something at him and pierced a hole in the screen. They stopped the show and tried to find out who did it. It wasn't me.

One of the highest points of my life was when I became 16 and got my driver's license. I thought that time would never come. I had been driving our old car for years when my parents were riding with me. They even let me drive a few times to Tuscumbia before I had license to drive. The day I became 16 years old, in 1954, I was at my brother's house in Sheffield and my sister-in-law Lorene let me drive their almost new Ford car to the Colbert County Courthouse in Tuscumbia to take my driver's test. I got my driver's license and was so excited to be able to drive in town legally. Since my brother Buddy was in the Army, Lorene was easy to persuade to allow me to drive their car for special trips around town. Driving meant I could have a date if my girlfriend's parents would let her go with me and I could use Buddy and Lorene's car. At this time Barbara was only 14 and, like me, she had never been on a date. We didn't have the nerve to ask if we could go out together for a long time, but the day finally came for us to go to a movie and to have a coke together. Barbara's parents reluctantly agreed to let her go only if we promised not to go to a drive-in theater. Of course, we said that we would not.

I walked over from my brother's house next door and chatted for a few minutes with her parents, Eugene and Myrtie Lee, and after being reminded to be careful and to be back before 10 o'clock, we walked to the car. We got in the car and were driving away up 14th Avenue when we heard something in the back seat. That's right, it was Carolyn, snickering like a nosy eight-year old stowaway. We laughed it off and took her back home to receive a good talking to by her mother and dad.

That first date was scary for me, I had not ever kissed a girl before and I doubt that Barbara had ever kissed a boy. But it didn't take me long to find out that she was a dynamite kisser. During the next couple of years, we went out together on Saturday nights, if I was not playing music somewhere. In those days there was almost nothing to do other than go to the movie and later stop by the Woody-Mac Drive-In for a curb service drink and hamburger. Our generation invented going "parking", where couples would go to a secluded place to park the car and smooch. I don't know if kids ever do that anymore, because we can see them out in public view doing more than we did while parking in our days. Our relationship became serious fairly quickly and we realized that we may be destined to be together throughout our lives. Kids did that a lot back then and called it "going steady". Most young people never dated more than one person before marriage. It's amazing how well that system worked. Couples very rarely divorced when they did marry. It was just the way we were raised and taught by our parents in those days. Marriage was a one man, one woman, for life institution. These values were set into the minds of all of us as we grew up and I'm glad they were; it's biblical teaching. My years in high school were filled with exciting events. I did everything but study my books. Most of the girls had boyfriends, some of them were older boys, and they never thought of me as anyone other than a close friend. They all knew that I had a girlfriend in Sheffield, although they had never met her. It turned out to be a good thing that Barbara and I lived in different towns because there is an old saying that "absence makes the heart grow fonder" and I believe it is true.

I always had jobs in the community, from chopping and picking cotton, to about anything else. I can remember one year I worked hard every day for a week just to go to the Northwest Alabama Fair in Florence and spend every dime. One winter I had the job of going to the Baptist church early on Sunday mornings and building fires in coal-burning stoves that were used for heating the building. They paid me $5.00 a week and I thought that was a good deal. I had already begun attending church there and found it was a good place to socialize and get to know people. I even worked as a volunteer in constructing a new church building on special days. Later, my parents and little sister began to attend the services on Sunday also. My older sister Vera and her husband Quinn attended the Methodist church, and some of my cousins attended the Church of Christ. I began to wonder, "Why does everybody need to go to a different church?" It was a very good question, but I never had the nerve to ask. I would go to church on Sunday nights also because daddy would let me drive the car to Church and back alone.

During those early years as a teenager, I had a strong inner feeling that God was taking care of me and directing my life. I had no reason to believe that He was looking out for me more than He did for others. Somehow, I was just aware of my vulnerability as a young person and wanted to do the right thing. Daddy once said, "Always do the right thing, and you know what that is." That was a profound statement, but I didn't fully understand its meaning.

I suppose all of us have that special person in our lives that we can identify as being the greatest influence to us. When I think about that person in my life, I don't need to give it a second thought. It is Willodine Malone, one of my teachers from elementary school and later on through high school. Her adult friends called her Billie and she was loved by every person who knew her. Mrs. Malone, as we all called her, had a certain love that was so encouraging and would make you want to learn. Her teaching went far beyond the regular academics and the appreciation for the arts and other things. She taught us life values that continue to influence my life today. I love Mrs. Malone as a person who played a major role in shaping my life. She was the one who encouraged me to stay in school when I became so disenchanted and wanted to join the U.S. Marines. I think I was just trying to punish myself to show my deep disappointment for not doing better as a student.

I had already picked up the enlistment papers that had to be signed by my parents because I was only 17 years old. The final decision was made when I carried the papers to my daddy and he said, "Boy, you better keep yourself in school, I'm not going to sign this paper." Thank goodness for that advice and firm parenting. If he had signed the papers, it would have destroyed my life and all the plans I had made for myself through the years. However, just to show him and to save face, I did join the Alabama National Guard with his permission. My best friend, Earl Dean White, and a few others joined up with me and it made us feel real grownup. It was not too long until I began thinking about the National Guard in the same way as I did about going to school earlier. I didn't like it, and it was getting in the way of my music life. I managed to muddle through the three year enlistment only to find out that it included another five-year stint in the U.S. Army Reserve. This was a killer for me. By the time the enlistment was up, I was out of high school, deeply into a musical career, married and the father of two children.

At one time in the early '60s, the 491st M.P. unit of which I was a member, was on stand-by alert with orders to the coast of Cuba. That time was scary for the whole country and, thank God, it worked out regarding the placement of Soviet missiles in Cuba just 90 miles off the U.S. shore.

CHAPTER FOUR

My junior and senior years in high school were filled with new adventures. I was active in going to every school event and entering talent shows around the region. Through my association with Tom Stafford of Florence I had established a wider circle of friends in the area of music and radio. This was about the time that Florence native, Sam Phillips, discovered Elvis Presley and others. One Saturday morning while I was finishing up a radio program at WLAY in Muscle Shoals, as I walked through the door of the studio into the lobby, I saw three guys waiting to be interviewed by the disc jockey at the radio station. I spoke to the one who appeared to be the leader of the group as if I were a big radio star and they were a wannabe group. After all, I had my own radio program and thought that was cool.

I said to the good looking guy as I walked up to him, "Hello, I'm Bobby Denton." and he said "Hi, Bobby, I'm Elvis Presley."

That name didn't ring a bell with me so then I said hello to the other two fellows who I later learned were Scotty Moore and Bill Black, who became famous as back-up players for Elvis. Later in the day I realized they were in town to perform at the Sheffield Community Center with a group of big country music stars. A couple of my friends and I went to the show just to see the Grand Ole Opry stars and never gave a thought about going to see Elvis and his little group, we had never heard of him. Little did we know that

Sam Phillips, who had started a small record company in Memphis, had booked Elvis on the show as a warm-up act for the big stars, to test the market for his new-found talent. The building was packed because we very seldom had big name entertainers come to the area. The audience never suspected that this stage show in Sheffield, Alabama, would go down in history as a big break for Elvis Presley on his way to becoming the King of Rock and Roll.

When Elvis, Scotty and Bill were introduced early in the program, he began singing "That's Alright Mama"; I had never heard a sound like it. I said to myself, "What is this?" With Elvis playing his acoustic guitar, Scotty playing his simple licks on the electric guitar, and Bill playing the stand-up bass, it was awesome. It was not country, it was not blues, and all I knew was that it was different and I loved it. By the time Elvis had finished his first song, the crowd was tearing the house down and he sang the song again. After the audience calmed down, he did the flip side of his new SUN record, "Blue Moon of Kentucky," an old Bill Monroe bluegrass song, but he didn't do it like Bill Monroe at all. It was a killer. It was so different, and it was actually what the young people at that point in time wanted to hear. We wanted something different from the music that was the mainstream country and pop, and Sam Phillips had found it. It was said after the program was over that one of the big stars, Webb Pierce said, "Don't ever book me again with this guy Elvis."

The next day after the show in Sheffield, all the local radio stations were playing the Elvis Presley records. Elvis had already made some in-roads on radio in Memphis, but we had never been exposed to his music in our area. Day by day the momentum built for him and within weeks his popularity had spread around the country. Within a year after the Sheffield show, SUN Records put on another show in Sheffield, and this time Elvis and his band were driving a new pink Cadillac car. The previous time he had been to the area and I spoke with him at the radio station, he was driving a 1953 Chevrolet. This latest trip to Sheffield, arranged by Sam Phillips and his brother Jud Phillips, a mastermind promoter, included the complete SUN Records gold mine of recording artists. It was a big deal and became known as the debut of several new stars. Johnny Cash was part of the group, along with Carl Perkins, the singer of the hit "Blue Suede Shoes." Carl was about to really hit the top with his record when he had an automobile accident that almost took his life and kept him from becoming a big superstar at that time. However, he managed to make a comeback within a few years. Elvis later recorded "Blue Suede Shoes" and most people never knew that Carl Perkins had the original record which I personally think was better than the Elvis version. With all these new talents being recorded and promoted by SUN Records, I thought that I may have a chance to be one of the people recorded by the upcoming company. One of my friends and I drove to Memphis one day hoping to meet Sam Phillips and maybe audition for him. After driving to Memphis, all we got to see was the famous studio where all the new recording artists had made their records. It was not overly impressive, just one big room with a control room adjacent to it with a large glass window overlooking the main studio. Most radio stations had studios as nice but it served the purpose it was intended to serve and I felt humbled by having visited the historic place for a few minutes.

Sam was out of town and he never called me back. Although I was deeply disappointed, I felt somewhat like the young salesman who knocked on his first door while hoping no-one was at home. After Sam Phillips had discovered Elvis he launched more artists who became famous, including Johnny Cash, Charlie Rich, Roy Orbison, and others. Later there was talk that SUN Records was preparing to come out with another new artist with blonde, curly hair, and a few people around home just knew it was going to be me. It was Jerry Lee Lewis who rocked the world with the song, "Whole Lot of Shaking Going On." Jerry Lee became a star fast and had several hit records; however, his rough lifestyle and his marriage to his very young cousin almost destroyed his career. The story broke while he was touring in Europe and the fans rebelled against him and boycotted his shows. Fans in the U.S. were about as defiant and his popularity plummeted.

Meanwhile, I was going into my senior year at school and having fun. My classmates were all good friends and we all got along well. Still nobody had a car except a few teachers and a girl named Patsy Logan, whose parents ran a store in Cherokee. They had bought her a brand new Buick convertible that year. We all piled into the car with Pasty almost every day to go into town and eat lunch. The high school was about two miles from downtown Cherokee. The last year in high school was my happiest of all. Although my grades continued to be on the low average, my classmates selected me to serve as associate editor for the 1957 yearbook "Hobachee" with Elizabeth Taylor, and Editor-in-Chief Ginger Thomason. The senior class also named Peggy Thomason and me as most attractive. I made most of the snapshots and action pictures of the individual football team members and did the draft layout for the book. One of my main helpers with the project was Donnie Kay Noe. We spent hours working together as we developed the entire yearbook, comprising all faculty and students from the seventh through the twelfth grade, along with all the sports and other activities of the school. Donnie Kay was like me; her boyfriend, Ernest Bechard, lived in Tuscumbia, and Barbara in Sheffield. We were among only a few who did not date people from the Cherokee area.

There were lots of girls in Iuka, Mississippi, where some of my friends and I went sometimes. It is about 12 miles west on Highway 72, so at times we went over to the Pan Am Café to have a hamburger and listen to the Jukebox. I also played music for a long time at a little theater in Booneville, Mississippi, on Saturday nights. Booneville is about 30 miles from Cherokee. I made most of the trips alone in my Dad's 1948 Chevrolet.

One day at school, in January of 1957, I was called to the principal's office to receive a phone call. I had no idea who could be calling me at school. I got to the phone excited and out of breath. The caller was James Joiner in Florence. He asked me if I would be interested in coming to see him in Florence to talk about recording for his new record company. I said, "Absolutely. I would love to come up to see you." We agreed on my coming to Florence on

Saturday. James and his family ran the Joiner Bus Line in Lauderdale County. The business was on Alabama Street in Florence and also served as the Greyhound Bus Station. The family had operated the bus line for years but I was not acquainted with them until I met James. James and his wife lived near the Town of Lexington in East Lauderdale County.

On Saturday, I hitched a ride to Florence to meet him at the bus station. There was no private area to meet so we went out into one of the buses that was parked in the rear of the bus station. He asked me a lot of questions about my plans when I finished school and if I would like to record the first record for the new company he and a few others were forming. This was a dream come true for me, so without question I said "yes." It was almost unbelievable to think about my actually making a record that would be played on the radio and hopefully sold in record stores. In the late '50s, kids relied on playing records and listening to the radio stations for their entertainment.

At that time, the older and larger 78 RPM speed records were going out of style, with the new 45 RPM records taking their place. The change-over was a little confusing at first, but kids didn't mind, they worked through the transition of the technology. All the new record players had the capacity to play 78 RPM and 45 RPM as well as the 33 1/3 speed. With the large hole in the center of the 45's, the players had an insert to fit down over the small spindle for the 78 RPM records. The regular spindle also was used for the new 33 1/3 speed long-playing albums with about 12 songs on them. Music in the '50s was the most exciting time ever, and we didn't realize the speed of modern technology although we had not seen anything yet.

The class of '57 continued to have fun enjoying our final year in school together with dreams and anticipation for the future. There was almost no talk among the class members about going to college. The way we were raised, getting a high school diploma would be about all we would ever need. It was easy to get a job around the area with all the large industrial plants and TVA employing thousands of people. These jobs meant having a good income with retirement and medical insurance for all employees and allowed them to have a much better way of life as they raised a family. We had never thought beyond society having a middle class that could afford new cars and nice houses. Most of us considered the world to be the "haves and have-nots." As far as I know, only a very few members of our class went on to college immediately after high school, although several of us went to college later on in life.

After the talk with James Joiner in the bus at the bus station, he went on to say he had written some songs and one of them, entitled "A Fallen Star," may be right for one of the songs we would need for my new record. He sang the song to me and he asked what I thought.

I immediately said, "It's great, I would love to record it." But after thinking about it later, I thought to myself, "what did he think an eighteen year old kid who would have killed to make a record would say?" I would have said that I loved it regardless if it was a good song or not.

Plans were quickly made to record the song with another of James Joiner's songs called "Carla," which I truly didn't like at all, but James never knew how I felt about the song. The next thing the baby recording company, TUNE Records, had to decide was where the songs would be recorded. The only professional recording studios in existence that we knew about were in Memphis and Nashville, which were used by the big recording companies. James and his associates decided that the only studio and tape recorder in the area that might do an acceptable job was at WLAY, the radio station where I had met Elvis earlier.

Even with the good studio and recorder, the setup and conditions were very primitive for recording a record to be produced and released for radio play and retail sales. The recording session was done in about an hour or two using three musical instruments and a local gospel quartet for backup. Of course, we didn't have the equipment to overdub mistakes, so the complete song had to be recorded all at the same time. Every instrument and vocal part had to be performed correctly throughout the entire song. There was no mixing of the levels or altering parts of the recording at a later time. Everything had to be done right at the same time. Also, the engineer who was the radio station disc jockey, Joe Heathcock, had to do his work and carry on the regular programming of the station at the same time. In order to give his full attention to our recording, he had to play an extra long record in order to oversee the two minutes and fifty-one second record we were recording. The same process was followed for the song going on the other side.

When the session was over, I was so proud to have had this great experience. However, I think all of us would have tried to do a better job had we known we were making history, the first master record recorded and distributed in the state of Alabama.

CHAPTER FIVE

In less than a month, we received the records from the pressing company in Nashville and copies were sent to radio stations all over the region, including the Birmingham area. The kids at school thought I was really something, especially the young girls; they were my biggest fans. The radio stations began playing the song, "A Fallen Star," and it was selling in local record shops. I was thrilled and could not believe what was happening to me. Could it be that I am going to be what I had always wanted to be in life? I was happy, and everyone loved me as a friend because I was just Bobby to them.

In just a few weeks after my record was released, I was notified that a big named artist had recorded my song. His record was recorded in Nashville with a major record company distributing it. When I heard the song on the radio, my heart almost broke. The song was recorded by Grand Ole Opry star Jimmy Newman. In a couple of weeks, another cover of the song was released by the popular singer Ferlin Husky, who also was with a major label company. And then, another version came out by the pop group, The Hilltoppers and later, another by the country music comedy singing duo Alonzo and Oscar. This was crushing to me and I could not believe that my simple little record was being overshadowed by all these other people who were being pushed by their big record companies.

At school, we were going into the final weeks of the year. I didn't let the situation regarding the record trouble me too much. I still had lots of things going on and TUNE Records was making plans for me to record my second record at an old empty movie house in Sheffield, the Ritz Theater. It was only a shell of a building with all the seating removed. The place was not the norm for a recording studio but by then James Joiner, with Kelso Herston, Walter Stovall, and a few others like Jimmy Johnson's uncle, Dexter Johnson, who was a master bass player and music expert, got the place ready to do the recording. A fellow named Charlie Stanfield, of Muscle Shoals, was an electronics buff and had purchased a lot of new recording equipment, microphones, and things to use in a studio. It was a hobby for him, and like most people he would do his hobby for almost nothing. The Ritz made a good hangout for us while things were coming together.

Meanwhile, things were winding down at school. The yearbook was printed and turned out good, and we were all excited about the coming graduation day. Finally, Friday evening, May 31st at 7:30 p.m. came and the 54 members of the class of 1957 received our diploma. I had never felt so happy. I could feel the love of my classmates and teachers, I could feel the love of my parents and members of my family, I could feel the love of my music, and I could feel the love of Barbara who had by now become a constant flame in my heart. It was a feeling of happiness and sadness at the same time. A sudden independence came over me that also brought to my mind that I was now grown up with responsibilities to deal with, and only 18 years old. I hit the ground running with my music every day.

The make-shift recording studio at the Ritz in Sheffield was ready to go, so James and the other guys set up the date for the session. James had a song of his in mind for me called "Lovers Paradise" which was a slow ballad love song and his brother-in-law, Walter Stovall, "Buddy" as we all called him, had written a faster paced song called "You'll Be the Last To Know." It turned out to be my favorite of the two songs. It was different in that Buddy played the ukulele in small parts of the song, which gave it a real good sound. Although the studio had better and more modern equipment, we still had to record as before, doing the song in one take. With the large area of the old theater, every instrument was spread out in different locations of the floor space and used a separate microphone, something that we didn't have for the first record at WLAY.

By now I had put together a real good band and we played all over the area and on WVOK radio station in Birmingham most Saturdays. On Saturday nights we were regulars at the National Guard Armory in Birmingham, which also was sponsored by WVOK. The radio station was a powerful 50,000 watts and was received all over Alabama. Our little group, all of us just kids, had a great time doing what we loved. I was like the daddy of the group of boys because I was just about to turn 19 years old. The band consisted of Peanut Montgomery, playing the electric lead guitar; Eddie Goodwin, playing the drums; and Ray Barger, playing the stand-up bass. Peanut later became very involved in the music business. He was a great songwriter and experienced success having big name recording artists record his songs. Peanut's greatest success came through the top selling artist George Jones recording his songs. He has had a lifelong career in music, as well as being successful in business in the Shoals area. Eddie, the drummer, after retiring from music, became a successful insurance executive. Ray, the bass player, later found employment in Tennessee where he and his wife raised their family. We continue to be good friends; however, time has a way of taking away the personal contact, but the love and memories will always remain.

My first car after graduation was a 1953 Plymouth four-door. I purchased it from a used car lot on 2nd Street in Muscle Shoals and I was very proud of it. I remember the car Elvis was driving the first time I saw him. It was a 1953 Chevrolet and had his name painted under the window on both sides in small letters. So, I thought that my name on the Plymouth would work nice for me too. The car would hardly hold the four of us with all the instruments. Ray's bass fiddle, in a canvas cover, was on a rack on the top. Eddie's drums and Peanut's amp were in the trunk. This meant that my and Peanut's guitars were inside the car with us.

This worked out well for around the area, but the trip to Birmingham was long and cramped for us. Buddy Stovall lived in Birmingham and helped me book shows for the band. We played at new car dealerships and other places, as well as the radio program and the Saturday night program at the National Guard Armory. I thought my car was fine until Buddy and James Joiner said to me that my name on the door of the '53 Plymouth was not very impressive and I should have a Cadillac to look more successful. That was easy for them to say; they were not going to make the payments and buy the gas as we played in Birmingham for about $50 a show. But the idea of driving a Cadillac sounded good to me, so the next week in Birmingham I went shopping around town for a big, four-door Cadillac with air conditioning and all the extras. After finding one, I made a tentative deal to trade for it but there was one problem: I didn't have any money or credit, so when I got home I asked my brother Buddy, if he would help me buy the car. Wanting to help me out, we went to the bank in Sheffield and he co-signed with me for the money to trade for a lavender 1955 Cadillac Fleetwood. The payments were $48 per month, and gas was about 25 cents a gallon. However, it was hard to realize much of a profit after paying the other boys a piddling amount for playing each show. But that car looked like a million dollars with the bass strapped on the top. It was just like the big stars in the music business, except they were making money, I suppose. As the months went by, and the road became longer, I found myself always away from home, and had very little time to see Barbara. I could feel that we were slipping apart.

In the summer of 1957, I was just beginning to become a low-level success as an eighteen-year-old singer in the newborn Rock and Roll music period. I was enjoying the lifelong dream of having a record play on the radio and for sale in record stores.

One night after playing a show with my little band at the National Guard Armory in Florence, Alabama, a friend suggested we take a couple of teenage girls who were big fans of ours to have a hamburger and coke. The good-looking sweet and innocent girls were eager to have the opportunity.

After the show, they piled into my 1955 Cadillac and we were off to a nearby drive-in restaurant. After the burger and coke, and being silly as teenagers could be, we headed for a parking spot somewhere up the Tennessee River from Wilson Dam at a boat ramp area.

At the time, I was in a break-up situation with my long-time girlfriend Barbara. I was deeply in love with her and was not looking for a new relaionship. However, I was also in love with my guitar. I suppose one could say I was hooked on music.

When we arrived at the parking spot, it was obvious that the space in the back of the car was a problem. My friend and the girl with him did not have enough room to see the moon's reflection on the river. The car trunk was full of drums and other equipment, and the back seat was also occupied by two guitars. So, at my friend's suggestion, I removed my guitar and sat it outside the car.

After a few minutes of moon-watching, my friend and I took the girls back to Florence because it was getting late. After dropping them off in Florence, I headed home to Cherokee about twenty-five miles west. When I arrived at my mom and dad's house, I began to remove the things that I never leave in the car overnight. Then, as though lightning had struck me in the head, I thought, "oh my Lord, my Lord, my Lord!" I'd left my guitar sitting on the ground at that boat ramp about thirty miles away and it was now 2:00 A.M.

I thought, "what can I do?" The gas guage on my car was on empty and there was no place open then to buy gas that late. It was seventeen miles from Cherokee to Tuscumbia, which was too far away to make it on an empty tank. I didn't have the nerve to wake my daddy at that time in the night and tell him the story and ask if I could use his old Chevy to dive back and get my guitar. That is what I should have done. However, I was ashamed of what I had done and was afraid of what his reaction would be. With hindsight, I think he would have understood. I went to bed but did not sleep until day break when I said good morning to my mom and dad as I rushed out of the house to the local service station and bought gas for my car. I was lucky not to get a speeding ticket driving back to the boat ramp, only to find that my guitar was GONE. My heart was broken as I thought, "that's what happens when you hoot with owls. . . you can't soar with eagles." Some early morning fisherman had made a real good catch.

Now, here is the very sad part. My guitar was a brand new Gibson-J45 that I had bought on monthly payments at Forbes Piano Company in Florence. It would be worth thousands of dollars today. I didn't have the money to buy another guitar and had to borrow one from friends until I could manage to buy another one.

This event has haunted me for forty-eight years. I have kept this bad memory all to myself. The good news is, within a few weeks following this, Barbara and I got back together and were married in November, 1957. "Till death do we part."

When one is 19 years old, it seems like time is dragging, and I was anxious to do more in the area of music. At one point, RCA Records wanted to buy my contract from TUNE, but they didn't want to sell. This was crushing to me also, because if I had gone with RCA my career would have been different, being with a giant company rather than the little local company with very small distribution and no funds to promote me. I felt trapped, and my dreams of becoming a star were dwindling.

The last performance we made was in Rome, Georgia, about 200 miles from home. Knowing this would be the last show for us was sad. I didn't know what the future held for me. I had not made plans for another career, other than music, to make a living. I was worried that Barbara would give up on waiting for me and we might not continue our plans together. We had already talked about being married when she finished high school. I was afraid and confused and I knew down deep that it was not going to work out. It was clear to me that I would not be able to do the music and work at another job at the same time. I had to decide which way I intended to go with my life. I gave it a lot of thought over the next few days. It's too bad that at that time I was not very close to God. Of course, I knew about Him, and believed in Him, but I had never given my life over to Him and to Christ as my Savior. Later I realized that God's purpose for me was being carried out in my life and He was guiding me to do His will.

God's love for us is far beyond our imagination in that He gave His Son to die for our sins and our only requirement is to believe in Him (Hebrews 11:6), repent from our sins (Luke 13:3; Acts 17:30), confess our faith in Him, believe Jesus is the Son of God (Romans 10:10; Acts 8:37), and be baptized for the forgiveness of our sins (Romans 6:4). And lastly, we must live according to His will. (Titus 2:12) I knew I had not done all these things and had not asked God to help me while I was going through all these life-changing experiences, but He loved me anyway and had other things in mind for me.

After thinking about my situation, I decided to get out of music and liquidate my assets in the business. First I told Peanut, Eddie and Ray, that I was quitting and wished them all well. Next I told Barbara, and at the same time asked if she would marry me. The only material assets that I had were the car and my guitar, and I owed more on the car than it was worth. A friend of mine who ran the used car lot where I had bought the Plymouth tried to sell it for me. He finally carried it to a used car auction out of town and sold it to the highest bidder. The resale value of the used '55 Cadillac that was previously owned by a small time rock and roll singer was not good. The car sold at a ridiculously low price and I paid the money to the bank and refinanced the balance on monthly payments. I sold my D28 Martin guitar back to Forbes Piano Company in Florence for about half the price I had paid for it. That guitar would be worth thousands of dollars today. Peanut, Eddie and Ray, continued to play music and were quickly drafted by other bands in the area. Hollis Dixon had a great band and so did Charlie Senn and Junior Thompson. Most of these boys who played music with all our bands went on to be professional musicians and were a part of the famous recording industry which later developed in the Muscle Shoals area. As for me, the biggest thing I had to do was swallow my pride and get a real job to make a living.

It was a big drop from being well-known in the area for most of my life and somewhat successful with music, to a $40 a week job with a termite company in Sheffield. Perhaps the hardest fall was from driving a Cadillac car down to driving a 1946 Ford. At first I thought my life was over and I did not have the courage to be in public with the shame I felt. I had always worked hard when I was growing up, but work was not what I had planned to do for a living.

Later, I managed to get a better job with a tiny newspaper in Sheffield, *The Muscle Shoals Morning Sun*. The job had a little better pay and more class; however, the company went out of business within a few months. My next job was with Stylon Southern Corporation in Florence; they made ceramic tile and paid about $70 per week. I felt better because several young men and women that I knew worked there. After working at Stylon only a few weeks, my life began settling down and I realized that I would have to work at a real job for the rest of my life. I tried to be content, to do as most of my school friends and I had been taught, get a job, get married, and have a family. So on November 22, 1957, Barbara and I were married in the same little house of her parents on 14th Avenue in Sheffield, with only our family in attendance. It was a simple service, with cake and punch, and then we were on our way for a weekend honeymoon because I had to be back to work on Monday.

Barbara was 17 and I was 19. We had already rented an upstairs apartment in Florence, and were excited about starting our new lives together. It was fun fixing up the apartment and we thought it was just what we needed, until we realized that both our families lived across the Tennessee River in Colbert County. Although they were only a few miles away, when a one-bedroom house in Sheffield became available, we moved in.

It was much better to have our own house and not have to climb stairs. Barbara spent her days fixing up inside the little house, and I was becoming more adapted to working in a manufacturing plant and trying to make ends meet living on a small income.

CHAPTER SIX

Over the next few months we were settling in as a married couple. I never wanted to go out in public much because of my continued embarrassment regarding my past experience in the music business. We mostly stayed close to the family and friends who accepted me for better or for worse. Two of our best friends were family also; Wayne and Sharon Green were our age and had married just a couple of months before us. Wayne was Barbara's first cousin, a quiet fellow who was very easy to get along with. Wayne was smart and could do about anything. Sharon was a pretty, energetic young lady who would later have a long career with the City of Muscle Shoals. Both of them always had a job and seemed to be more prosperous than we were; however, they always had fun doing things with us and we with them. Some of the most memorable times were driving in the snow in my old 1946 Ford and spinning around in the street. One night after a big snow, we asked them to spend the night with us. They said they would love to but where would they sleep with only a one-bedroom house. We considered the couch or a pallet on the floor, but that would not have been very private. So, after exploring all the options, they decided on a large storage closet only big enough to accommodate a one-person cot that we had. It was so funny, and we all had fun being together. I believe Wayne and Sharon enjoyed the closeness of the cot also.

Another couple was also a family member of Barbara's. They were Ralph and Janell Montgomery. Although Janell was only a couple of years older than Barbara, she was her aunt, a sister of Barbara's Dad. They were ahead of us and were already beginning their family, and Ralph had a good job. Times were not easy then, but we were happy and had more things than we did growing up.

After being married only four months, Barbara became pregnant. This was a shocker that we didn't need at that time. With no medical insurance, and no money, we were afraid for our uncertain future. However, as most young people, we didn't worry much about what would happen to us because being young one has a feeling of unconcern in these matters, more than we do as we get older.

I was beginning to adjust to life without being involved with music, however, my mind continued to flash thoughts of what I could have done better. And then one day, without any prior warning, I was called by the new owner of radio station WLAY, who said that he and another associate would like to come to my house and talk with me. Of course I said "yes" and the meeting time was set. I had no idea what this was all about. They came to our little house on 11th Street in Sheffield and began talking to me about plans they had for a new record company, and what they wanted to offer me. It seemed their plan was very well thought out and would be a great success. They told me a record company was being formed by WLAY, two optometrists, and my friend Kelso Hurston, along with the legendary promoter, Judd Phillips. The company would be called Judd Records. They wanted me to be their first project and even had the song picked out to be on the first record. The story went on and on and they said the song would be featured on the popular Dick Clark Saturday night show on ABC television from New York. By now my head was spinning and I could not believe what they were offering me. They already had the appearance booked on the TV program and plans to record the song. Judd Phillips was a master promoter, and was known throughout the nation by record distributors as well as radio and TV contacts. Judd had a good track record for his talent in promoting artists from

Elvis to several others that his brother Sam had recorded on SUN Records. This proposal was by far the biggest opportunity that anyone could ever imagine. It was hard to believe that I was their choice for this chance of a lifetime.

My problem was I had already quit music and I was married. Besides that, we were expecting a baby in a few months. I had never heard of an opportunity like I was being offered. They were planning to record in Nashville at the famous Owen Bradley studio, with the best musicians in the business.

I knew Barbara was not excited about my getting back into music, I could see it on her face. I knew she must have been thinking, "Well, here we go again, Bobby gone and even worse, this time I'm home alone and pregnant." I could understand that and I was tempted to just say, "No thanks" and not take the out-of-this-world opportunity. Every questionable scenario as to why I couldn't do it was countered by the reply "We will do it" or "That's all right, we'll take care of it." They said that Barbara could go to Nashville with me to make the record and go with me to New York for the TV program. When she said, "I am beginning to show, and I don't have the proper clothes to wear," they said, "We will buy you a complete new wardrobe." Then we wondered about my job and how we could continue to pay our bills. They said, "We will pay your salary from the time you leave your job, until you start making the big money later on." It seemed that there was nothing we could say to discourage their determination to have me do this project.

The conversation went on for hours, and we decided to think about it and meet again the next day. At the second meeting, more of the details were revealed and questions asked. They had plans for a record promotional tour after the TV show that would last about six weeks, covering every major city from the entire east coast, west through Oklahoma. They had a customized bus complete with every amenity, including a phone, restroom, and sleeping accommodations. Jerry Lee Lewis had just completed a similar tour on the same bus. The plans also stipulated that I would appear on the TV program in early September, on the first weekend of the new school year. The set was already planned for the new song that I was to perform, entitled "Back to School," which was written by Claunch and Maynard of Memphis.

After doing the TV program, Barbara would fly home while I continued on the tour. Never in my wildest dreams could I have imagined a chance such as this. I was in shock and spellbound, but I could see Barbara was not convinced that this would be good for her. However, I believe she also knew this was a very big deal and if she stood in my way it could affect our marriage later. Both of us knew this was a chance of a lifetime and it was just too good to pass up. So we said yes to the proposal made by the company. The next thing I had to do was give my notice to Stylon that I would be quitting the job in two weeks. In the meantime, a date was set for the record to be recorded in Nashville.

Judd Records asked Florence native Buddy Killen, who was the Vice President of Tree Publishing Company, to produce the session and arrange for the players and background voices. At this point they didn't have the side "B" song selected for the record, so when we arrived in Nashville on the day of the session we went to Buddy Killen's office at Tree Publishing Company, which was the same publisher for my record with TUNE Records.

Tree Publishing had skyrocketed within the last year with big hit songs like "Heartbreak Hotel" by Elvis. We previewed several songs, trying to find anything that would work out for the other side of "Back to School," which they thought would be the hit song after singing it on the Dick Clark Show. After hearing several demos, Buddy said, "See what you think about this song, "Sweet and Innocent," written by two boys from North Alabama, Rick Hall and Billy Sherrill, who then lived in the Hamilton area. He played the simple demo for us and I said, "That's it, I think that is a good tune, let's do it." And so Buddy put his creative mind in action and began imagining what he wanted the two songs to sound like and who he wanted to play the music. It was like a miracle that he hired the very best people in Nashville to play on the record. They were all right there in town and available to play. Buddy Killen knew his way around the music business and was one of the brightest music people I have ever known. Later, I found out that the nice fellow who got me a coke during the session, and played the saxophone, was the music legend Boots Randolph, and the quiet clean-cut guy who played the piano was Floyd Cramer, who later became popular around the world with his song, "Last Date." Every person who played on that session was the best, even the background voices were the Jordanaires, who became famous performing with Elvis Presley, and a girl singer named Anita Kerr, who headed up the very popular Anita Kerr Singers. The Owen Bradley studio was more advanced than the studios we had used with TUNE Records, and was considered the best in the business at that time. Everyone was happy with the results of the new recording. The technology allowing track recording was just coming to the Nashville studio, but we still recorded with everyone in the same room as we had done in the makeshift studio in the Shoals.

After the recording session was over, Barbara and I rode back home to Sheffield with two co-owners of Judd Records, Dr. Robert Maxwell and Dr. Alvin McClendon of Florence. I was so happy with the recording session. It was the best record by far that I had ever made. I loved both sides of it and could hardly wait for the release date. There were still lots of things to do. We went shopping in Memphis and purchased Barbara several new outfits to wear to New York and afterwards while she was expecting the baby. Meanwhile, I worked my last few days at the Stylon plant. All the people at work were excited about my going to New York and being on national television. As the September 6th date came nearer, Barbara and I were growing more anxious about leaving and saying goodbye to our family and friends.

One of Barbara's aunts, Peggy Simpson, and her husband John, had us over to their house for supper one night to wish us well. They gave me a Bible to carry with me on my trip. The local newspaper ran articles about the coming event, and the people of the Shoals area were waiting to see their local boy on network tele-vision. We left Florence on the bus on Thursday and traveled all that day and the next night. Making the trip with us on the bus was

Judd Phillips, Alvin McClendon, and James Phyfer, a nice black fellow from Sheffield who became my best friend over the next several weeks. James looked out for me and made sure my clothes were clean. He also served as an assistant for everyone on the Big Apple trip, as well as the six week tour that followed the TV show. Upon our arrival in New York, at the Manhattan Hotel, we must have looked like a group of bums after traveling all that distance, and Barbara showing greatly by then. But it was fine because we didn't see a single person we knew.

The group checked into the hotel and were assigned our rooms. We rested during the day because I had my first meeting with the TV producers and Dick Clark later that afternoon at the ABC studio, about three blocks up on 44th Street. Taking a taxi to the studio, I went inside, and every guest to appear on the program was seated waiting for instructions and to meet Dick Clark. When Dick came in he welcomed us and asked that we stand as the producer called our names. When my name was called, I stood up and Dick Clark commented, "Oh good, a teenager." Next we were instructed as to what format the show would have and some things we should know about being on a big TV program. First, the producer said that this program was sponsored by Beechnut Gum and was the most watched TV program in the nation that year. He told us not to be nervous because only 44 million people would be watching. I thought to myself, "Man, this is a long way from Cherokee, Alabama." After the briefing, a man said I would have to join the TV and Movie Actors Union before the performance and to be on other major TV stations around the country. So, the record company paid my dues of $120. The minimum union pay for the appearance was $155.00. After that, I was good to go back to the hotel. I still have the W-2 form.

The next day, we had two rough rehearsals and a tweaking of the program timing. This was September 6th, 1958. Everything on TV then was live, they didn't even have video tape; that came along later. A few of the big shows had already begun to film programs, but ABC had not begun doing that on this program. They even rehearsed the commercials and camera shots. I had a special-made set just for me. I wore a plaid shirt with blue jeans and white buck shoes. In late afternoon, before the live program was to air, we had a dress and camera rehearsal, with a full live audience. Then that audience was replaced by all new people who were waiting outside to see the show. Of course, I had to go upstairs to have the makeup person give me the usual non-glare facial treatment, which is standard for TV. Barbara came to the dress rehearsal and afterwards went back to the hotel to see the program on TV. The program came off without a glitch and I was so proud of myself and for the opportunity to have this experience.

CHAPTER SEVEN

By the time the TV program was over, I had gotten to know the other entertainers who performed with me. I quickly realized that I was in extremely prestigious company. Among the stars appearing were the famous Ruth Brown, and the great singer Tommy Edwards, who recorded "It's all in the Game," which later became a top seller around the country. At that time in the late '50s, with rock and roll music on the rise, the radio airwaves were saturated with new groups of performers who could shoot to the top of the charts in a matter of weeks through the relatively new medium of television and the even more popular radio.

One of the most memorable things that occurred at the event came as we were exiting the TV studio. The studio was located on 44th Street, just off Broadway, near Times Square. The location was in the same vicinity of several Off Broadway theatres. The pedestrian traffic was so crowded the police department would close off 44th street to automobile traffic when the theatres were active. They even notified us at the program briefing that we would need our own security. The police were on foot and horseback to manage the crowds of people. As we exited a side door of the TV studio, I saw the street completely packed with people and teenagers screaming as we made our way on to the sidewalk. I had never seen anything like it. Besides the people who had filled the TV studio and were waiting outside to see us coming out, there was a play ending just across the street from the door we were exiting. The street was jammed with yelling kids and excited fans pressing against each other. Then I heard some guy shout loud from across the street, standing on a fire plug, "Who is it?" and the young girls around me shouted back, "It's Bobby Denton!" to which the man replied, "I have never heard of him." That was a big deal being in New York City and fans surrounding me like that; it was almost unbelievable. As I was making my way through all the people, I wondered to myself, "Where in the world is James? He's supposed to be here with me." Then I looked back behind me and saw James signing autographs for the kids. They didn't know who was who; they just knew we were all coming out of the TV studio. Finally, I made my way down the street to the Manhattan Hotel with the feeling of success that I had never experienced before.

Our entire group from home that came to New York to support me on the program was waiting at the hotel with Barbara to congratulate me for the good job they said that I had done. Everyone felt the new record would do well for us. Later, we all went to the famous restaurant Sardi's for dinner and I could not believe the bill's total was $120 for the group. It would be $1,000 or more today.

The next day, Barbara and three of the record company owners, with their wives, flew back to Muscle Shoals. It was sad to see them leave me in the largest city in the country, alone. Barbara had never flown before and I was worried about how she would make the trip. With them gone, that left only Judd Phillips, Alvin McClendon, James and the bus driver to finish the long tour with me.

After the TV program, the New York radio stations began playing my record and the area record distributor ordered 70,000 copies.

We continued around the city for a couple of days to meet big named disc jockeys.

I wanted to do some sightseeing while we were there, so James and I walked around Manhattan, up and down Broadway, to see everything. I had never dreamed of a 24-hour a day city, but that's what it was, with people going and coming around the clock.

While walking along Broadway, we passed a shoe-shine stand sitting back in a little area at the edge of the sidewalk. So, James and I decided to get our shoes shined. As I was sitting in the shoe-shine chair, I could not believe my ears. The shoe-shine man had a small radio sitting on a shelf and one of my songs, "Sweet and Innocent," began playing on the radio station. I was about to freak out, and I told the guy, "Hear that song? That's me!" All he said in reply was, "Uh, huh." After that unforgettable experience, James and I went on to the Empire State Building and viewed the city from its top. I have been back to New York once since that time, but my first visit will always be the most memorable.

The emphasis placed on the theme of back to school was the main reason I was booked on the Dick Clark program, and was to take advantage of the timing for record buying kids. Although I had sung the song "Back to School" on national television, the radio stations all liked the other side of the record better and were playing "Sweet and Innocent." It was the same everywhere we went. When we got to Boston, "Sweet and Innocent" was one of the top 40 tunes on the radio charts. As we made our way all over the New England states, my record was popular. We continued on through the mid-west and into Minnesota, Oklahoma, Texas, New Orleans, Mobile, and then home to the Shoals area. In every large city, I met the record distributors and did radio and television inter-views.

Within a few weeks after the New York trip, RCA Records contacted Judd and offered to buy my recording contract, along with the master tape of "Sweet and Innocent." But Judd Records did not take their offer. Within another two weeks, RCA released a new record by the former SUN Record artist, Roy Orbison, sing-ing "Sweet and Innocent". The song was later recorded by Donny Osmond and was a very big hit. I had recorded a later version for Rick Hall in Muscle Shoals, but it just turned out to be the demo for Donny. That was my second time to have a chance to be with RCA. I was not too disappointed because Judd Records had given me everything anyone could have ever asked.

Finally, it was good to be home after such a long and tiring trip. By now Barbara was really getting a large tummy. According to my agreement with the record company, I could stay home with her until after the baby was born. Then I would be going on a tour, this time with Jerry Lee Lewis and other entertainers who were up coming artists. The tour was called the Dick Clark Tour. We did live shows which were booked mainly in the southern states.

During my stay at home, there were lots of things going on. By this time it was evident that my records, "Back to School" and "Sweet and Innocent," were about to run their course and were not going to be big hits. The record company had already made plans for me to go to Houston, Texas, and record my next release. I was not asked for my opinion regarding this choice of the recording location, and did not understand the strategy of going to Houston rather than going back to Nashville and allowing Buddy Killen to produce the second record as he did with the last one. I was disappointed about the decision and the fact that very little planning had been done in the selection of the songs to be recorded. This should have been a well-thought-out process, considering the success we had with the first record and the excellent exposure I had received over the last few months around the country. However, I suppose the final decision was made by Judd Phillips and he trusted the people in Texas who ran the studio and produced the session. One positive thing about the studio was it had the latest equipment, which allowed what is called overdubbing and recording on different tracks. Although in my mind, it was still not Nashville and did not have the professionalism and good players that we had before.

The session date was set and plans were made to make the trip to Houston. Ironically, my mother's sister, Aunt Flora, and her husband Connie, lived in Houston and owned a dry cleaning business. So I thought it would be nice to take my Mom and Dad and little sister Cala to Texas with Barbara and me. They had never been far away from home and it would be a good experience for them. By that time I had a better car, a 1956 Buick, so we all took off. The songs that were decided for the new record were not as powerful as the others I had recorded in Nashville, but what did I know, I was just thrilled to be making records.

The song that was to be the "A" side of the record was "Lovers Plea," written by two people from Texas, Schular and Broussard, and published by Longhorn Music Incorporated. The other song, "I'll Always be Yours," was a song that Tom Stafford and I had written. I had already formed a publishing company called Bobby Denton Music and was an affiliate of BMI (Broadcast Music Incorporated), the leading company for songwriters and music publishers at that time, so I was the publishing company also. After recording the new record, we made our way back to Alabama. My Mom and Dad and Cala had a good time with the visit and the experience of seeing a big city and all the sights in between.

When we got back home I still had some time on my hands before the baby was to be born. I would be joining the Dick Clark Tour in just a few weeks. Much of my time was spent working with Tom Stafford trying to put together a recording studio upstairs over his Dad's drugstore on Tennessee Street in Florence. The studio would be for recording demo records of songs to pitch to record companies and other publishers. All I knew about studios was what I had observed seeing the inside of others, and that they needed to be as sound proof as possible. That was a big job and I began work trying to do it. I went to every big grocery store in the area and asked them for the old carton dividers that were used to ship eggs to the stores. They were porous, soft cardboard with the little indentions on them where the eggs sat while being shipped. They were about 16-inches square and perfect for the walls and ceiling of the studio. I had blisters on my hands from using a staple gun to install the hundreds of egg cartons needed to cover the big room.

Later, we went to Nashville and purchased a tape recorder and a few items for the studio. It was not as good as the professional studio that was used for my latest records, but we thought it would do fine. We went to Nashville in my '56 Buick and returned the same day, excited about the recording studio above the City Drug Store, which quickly became the number one hangout for all the boys around town who were aspiring to play music and write songs. We had fun experimenting with the equipment and being together. My being married made me a little different from the others because they could play music and hang out as long as they wanted, but my responsibility as a husband, and soon-to-be father, compelled me to get home at reasonable times.

The time for Barbara's delivery was coming closer and closer. I knew she was miserable and scared facing this first time experience of giving birth. Finally, the time came and we went to Colbert County Hospital, which is now Helen Keller Memorial Hospital. It seemed like forever waiting for the baby. Back then the doctors did not have the technology to know the sex of the unborn. We were excited and wondered whether it would be a boy or a girl. We didn't really feel strongly about that aspect as long as the mother and child were all right.

Our strong and healthy baby girl was born and we were so happy. Becoming a parent brings on a feeling of serious responsibility almost immediately; it is not just we the couple anymore, but the child also who is solely dependent upon its parents to care for her. The baby was born on December 21st, 1958. She was so sweet and beautiful. We had already talked about a name, but no decision had been made because of not knowing if the baby would be a boy or a girl. So within a short time after the birth we named her Juliana Lee. The middle name was used to honor Barbara's mother who had the same middle name.

Christmas was just a couple of days away and we went home with our new gift from God, our little Julie. With the help of Barbara's mother and dad, and the other members of our families, we made it fine. Friends and family had showered us with gifts for the new baby, which helped us a lot. We had an old, used washing machine, but did not have a clothes dryer, so the diapers had to be dried on a rack inside when the weather was too bad to hang them outside. Little Julie was a prize and not a lot of trouble to care for. She began sleeping all night within a few days and was seldom sick. Our little family was content being at home. Although we didn't have a nice home and fancy car, we had love for each other. All the while, in the back of my mind, I remembered the agreement with the record company and that I would have to leave soon to meet the others on the tour. Within a few days I received the call from them that I would be picked up by a driver and carried to meet the group and tour with them. I didn't have a good feeling about leaving Barbara and Julie. I had grown up a lot over the last year and my priorities had begun to change, but when the car came to our little house I had to go; I had no choice.

CHAPTER EIGHT

The tour was not as I expected. It was not fun. I felt out of place and didn't hang out with the others much. After a couple of weeks, I felt a choice would have to be made regarding my future. This was what I had always wanted to do, but it wasn't working out. As I thought about my options, I knew that whatever my final decision was, it would be life changing. I was homesick and miserable living on the road. It became clear that this was not the life for a person with a wife and young child at home. However, if I chose to quit the tour and go home I would feel guilty for not fulfilling my commitment to the record company, and if I continued with the others I would not be doing the right thing for my family.

After pondering my situation for a few days, my feeling did not change much. I called Barbara one day and I could hear in her voice the desire for me to come home, but she never said she wanted me to come home. I just knew that's where I needed to be, for better or for worse. I told her about my dissatisfaction with the tour and that I would be coming home soon. I told the road manager that I wanted to quit the tour, so the next day one of the employees of the company had to travel back to Florence for some reason and I got a ride home with him. My chance in music would be over now. The one thing that I had always wanted to do would be gone forever and I didn't know how I would handle it. Somehow, the saying "do the right thing, and you know what that is," kept sticking in my mind. I truly felt that I was doing the right thing although the future would be rough and rocky for me. Once again I had to deal with the stigma of being unsuccessful in music, swallow my pride, and continue on with my life.

After I had left home to go on the tour, Rick Hall and Billy Sherrill joined up with Tom Stafford and began operating the studio above the City Drug Store that I had worked so hard helping to get together.

The next year was hard for us. I couldn't find a job anywhere around home. We went to visit Barbara's aunt and uncle in Memphis, Bess and Grady Stewart, to spend a few days looking for a job, but I was not successful. A friend of mine called and said he knew of a job in sales located in Corinth, Mississippi, which is about 45 miles west of Muscle Shoals. I applied for the job and we moved into a small duplex apartment in Corinth. We were in a strange town with very little chance of success. However, there was some benefit to living in an area where I was not well known. As the weeks passed, I did a lot of thinking about what was going to become of me and my life. I needed to do something to have the inner peace inside that I wanted so badly. Barbara's parents were Christians and very dedicated to God. Their faith had influenced her greatly as she grew up and she would sometimes ask me about going to church. I had never spent time studying the Bible and seldom attended church. However, as I became more mature I could feel the need to do something to better obtain God's blessings and guidance in my life.

One morning a man came by our house to ask if we had any laundry or dry-cleaning that he could pick up. He was the owner of the business so pickup and delivery was a part of the company's service. He was nice. As we chatted for a few minutes, he asked me where we went to church. I told him that Barbara was a member of the Church of Christ but we didn't attend church. I then went on to tell him that I might be interested in becoming a Christian someday. He invited me to come by to talk with him and the minister of the Foot Street Church of Christ there in town. Later that day I went by the church building to talk about what one must do to be saved. After talking with them for a long time, I accepted Christ as my Savior and was baptized for the forgiveness of my sins. After that experience I felt a load had been lifted from me, and it seemed I was now prepared to deal with whatever problem I would be confronted with in life.

Within a few weeks my old friend, and Barbara's uncle, Ralph Montgomery, contacted me and asked if I would be interested in coming back home to work for him and his partner. They had a new business manufacturing aluminum windows and doors. They asked if I would travel around the region in Alabama as a sales representative for the small company. Ralph said they would pay my expenses and mileage for my car, along with a salary of $75 a week. I quickly accepted the offer and we moved back to the Shoals. We felt a lot better being closer to our families, especially Barbara's parents, who loved little Julie and helped us take care of her.

Before going to Memphis and Corinth, I had already made application for a job at several places around home with no luck receiving an offer. I remembered the last day I had worked for Stylon in Florence. The plant manager said to me, "Bobby, if you ever need another job with us let me know and I will see what we can do." One night, after calling on every building supply and hardware store in the small town of Pell City, Alabama, I called Barbara. She said the man from Stylon called and asked if I would like to come back to work doing the same job I had done before. I could not wait to take them up on their offer the next day. The only way to describe how I felt would be to compare myself with the story of the prodigal son in the Bible. He left home and had a wondering experience that didn't work out and came back home. When I left my job over a year before, I never thought I would ever be so excited to have it back again. I had experienced a lifetime of things some folks would have loved to have done, but I found out for myself what the full-time music business was really like and the price of experiencing it.

Although I was extremely thankful to have my old job back, I knew it would not provide the income that I would like to have in order to provide for my family and have a better life. I had applied at Ford Motor Company's local plant that had failed to give me a chance before. Because I was interested in music, they thought I would not stick with the job, and they were probably right in their thinking. However, now I was serious about a job with Ford and every few days I made contact with them about hiring me. After several months, Ford called me and I went to work for them. We thought this was as good as it gets, making over $100 a week and good benefits. I became well adapted to the job and made friends with all my co-workers.

As time went by, I realized that to have a better job in the plant I would have to prepare myself to qualify for it. The best job in the plant, in my opinion, was that of quality control inspector. I noticed those guys walking around wearing nice clean clothes. They would check charts at the machines and look over the auto parts that were being made. I decided that job was what I would like to have. After asking questions regarding the position, I was told that I could only get the job when an opening occurred, and the person who scored highest on the test was given the position. This was my new goal, to have the quality control inspector job.

I began staying over after work to study the instruments and gauges that were used. I would have to be able to properly read the parts blueprints and dimensional requirements to do the job. I stayed over at work studying these things one or two nights per week, preparing for the next opening. Finally, a position came open and I knew I was ready for the challenge. I scored 100 on the test; however, another fellow also made a perfect score, so he was given the job because he had been with Ford longer. This was so disappointing, but another job came open within a few months and this time it was mine. I remained on that job for more than 10 years before resigning in 1971 to devote full time to the little business which I had established.

With the good job at Ford, and things going well, Barbara and I were happy raising our young family. On January 19th, 1960, our second baby was born, 13 months after Julie was delivered. This time we had a boy and we named him Bobby Michael. Everyone always called him Mike. 1960 was not a good year for the automobile business and Ford began to lay off workers, but I was among the lucky ones and was never laid off from work.

When little Mike was just about a year old, we noticed his eyes jumping and thought something was wrong. He was fitted with glasses at that young age and could see much better. Later, he developed another problem with his eyes crossing sometimes. We carried him to Memphis to an ophthalmologist and Mike later had surgery on his eyes. That was a frightening experience for us, and required several trips to Memphis because of complications. Little Mike was tough and he did well coping with his eye problem as he grew up and began going to school.

With Julie and Mike only 13 months apart, Barbara had her hands full, at first especially. She was dealing with two babies in diapers at the same time, carrying one and leading another. The two were almost like twins and loved each other immensely. The older Julie was always the little care-giving mother of the two. Julie and Mike loved their grandparents, especially Barbara's mom and dad. They enjoyed being at their house and the grandparents loved for them to be there.

After renting houses all around town, we purchased our first house on Highpoint Street, just east of Muscle Shoals, off River Road. It was a new, one street subdivision of small brick homes. The house was nice; however, by today's standards it was not great at all. We had three bedrooms, all hardwood floors, and one bathroom with ceramic tile. It had nice kitchen cabinets, but no built-in appliances. The house had a single car carport, which was popular then, and electric heat; no central heat and air. We thought the house was very nice compared to the others we had lived in since being married. The total cost of the house was just over $6,000, and the payments were $67 per month, including property taxes and insurance. The house was convenient to the Ford plant, but was not ideal for going into town, about five miles away. Within a year we had become tired of the inconvenience of driving into town and only having a small yard, which would be the same as if we were living in town. So, we sold the house to a friend at Ford and bought another older house in a nice established neighborhood in Sheffield. Then in a couple of years, we purchased another new house in Muscle Shoals on Tuxedo Avenue. By that time, we realized that the location of schools was a factor. Muscle Shoals was a fast growing town and had new schools. Highland Park Elementary School was just a few blocks from our house on Tuxedo, so Julie started to school one year, and Mike followed the next year. Although we had only one car, it worked out well being centrally located.

We continued to maintain close contact with Barbara's parents and attended church with them in Sheffield. My dad and mom had built a nice little house in Cherokee and were excited about having a better house for themselves and Cala. I remember daddy talking about when he signed the papers for his 20-year mortgage. He was 60 years old and the lender at the bank said, "Now Mr. Denton, I'm expecting you to personally bring us your last payment when you are 80." He had a good laugh with the banker when he made the final payment 20 years later.

Barbara and I began to think about another child since Mike was now five years old. Things were going well with us and we thought another child would be good, and three children would be a nice size family. Julie and Mike were good little kids and got along so well together. When we told them we were going to see if God would send us a little baby, they were so excited.

When we announced to our families that we were expecting, my brother Buddy and his wife Lorene were very surprised because they had just found out about Lorene being pregnant also. They already had their son Mark, who was four years old at the time. We were all looking forward to the new babies joining the family. My brother Johnny and his wife Doris already had two boys, Robert and Steve. My sister Vera and her husband Quinn had a boy and a girl, George and Beth Susan. So the family was growing fast. Lorene delivered just about two weeks before Barbara, but the big surprise was Lorene had twin girls. They were named Tina and Gina. They were tiny, but healthy.

Then came our little baby boy Roger. He was so beautiful and was born on my birthday, August 13. Little Roger was so lovable and special in many ways. Julie and Mike were happy to have him as their baby brother.

CHAPTER NINE

When Roger was born, I was 27 years old and Barbara was 25. We realized that we were grown adults and began thinking differently about family and life. Like most young couples who marry early without a good income, it took us a few years to see the need of planning for our economic future. Although my job at Ford was good, we seemed to be always just short of having money left after the bills were paid. We were not living beyond our means; I think we just didn't manage our money as well as we should have. It seemed that from my teenage years I always had to have more than one job, even if I didn't get paid for doing the second one.

In the middle '60s a lot of people began using citizen band radios as a hobby. It became a national craze by mostly young men to have a two-way radio at their home and in their car. The sport was to have the best signal and tallest antenna around to talk with others in the area and sometimes in other states. This fad was right down my alley because of my life-long fascination with antennas. As my friends became interested in CB radios, I would always be first to help them install their antenna. These antennas became higher and higher with the use of towers to mount them on. Before long all my spare time was consumed with helping friends install their towers and antennas. I, with a friend of mine at Ford, began doing this work as a side job and charged for the service. At first we installed CB radio antennas and then TV antennas became the main source of business. Because of the long distances from our area in Northwest Alabama to the major cities with TV stations, one had to have a TV antenna high above the ground to receive a clear TV picture from the stations in Birmingham, Nashville and Memphis. The Shoals area had a UHF TV station which began operating in the mid '50s. Decatur had a station also, but the "UHF" (ultra high frequency) stations were extremely short range. With cable TV in its infancy, and not available outside the highly populated areas, the use of a good antenna was necessary.

Within a year, the little part-time TV antenna business became bigger and more demanding. I always had a co-worker at Ford who wanted to make extra money working with me. We worked at night at Ford and most all day installing TV antennas. The little hobby turned into a full-time business over the next several years, which was another dream come true for me as a boy. The job was dangerous, and I had several very close calls through the hazards of working high above the ground building towers, and always around electric wires.

One day in the early '60s, I was almost killed while installing a TV tower and antenna. It happened at a home on the side of a lake that had power lines running almost directly over the house. The man working with me was on the tower and I was on the ground. As I pulled a wire to him, the wire came in contact with a high voltage power line. I was sent tumbling several feet and was unconscious for a few minutes. The 7,200 volts of electric power went through my body, burning my hands, although I was wearing gloves, and then came out of the heel of one foot, making a hole. An ambulance was called and I was taken to the hospital in Florence. Back then the communities did not have emergency rescue services. There was not even an ambulance as we know them today. A local funeral home was sent to get me and take me to the hospital in a hearse they used to carry dead people. Not to mention, they had no life-saving skills or equipment. I was treated at ECM Hospital in Florence and the next day transferred to the hospital in Sheffield where I remained for three days.

After the accident happened I was told by people who had knowledge regarding electric shock that if I were to experience this event 100 times, I would be killed 99 of them. I was thankful to God for my survival and returned to work at Ford in two weeks.

Little Roger was growing and the family was happy to have the new baby boy, as well as Lorene and Buddy's twin girls. Roger had an operation when he was one-year old for a hernia, but recovered well. One night a few months later, while he was suffering from a normal childhood cold and fever, he stopped breathing. All I knew to do was push on his back with my hands while he lay on his stomach. I pushed down on his body and then released the pressure back and forth as we prayed for him to take a breath of air. After a short time, he took in air when I released the pressure on his body. He then began breathing normally. By that time Barbara's mom and dad arrived at the house to help us. They stayed with Julie and Mike while we carried Roger to the emergency room at the hospital. They found nothing wrong and said he had experienced a very high fever and his body had just shut down as a result.

The next year we traded our house on Tuxedo Street for another new house a few blocks away on Highland Avenue in Muscle Shoals. In those days one could trade houses like trading cars. The new house was more expensive, but it had several things that we liked much better. It had central heat and air-conditioning, two baths, and built-in appliances. All the new streets in Muscle Shoals were just being developed and the area where our houses were located did not yet have paved streets. The town was just beginning to develop, with new subdivisions which required infrastructure like paved streets, water and sewage lines. Then it was different from today, because the subdivision developers did not install these things, and the City contracted for the work to be done. The City did bond issues and assessed the property owners to repay the bonds. Now the developers pay for these things and add the cost to the sale of the house.

The downside of buying a new home in a new subdivision was that almost everyone was a young couple raising a family like we were. Most of the home-owners had two or three kids, and when considering several homes on a street, the number of kids was sometimes overwhelming. I came home one afternoon and found bicycles all over the driveway and kids everywhere. The kids for the most part were nice; however, with that many on the street there were always disagreements among them causing unrest with the parents.

We then began thinking about moving again, and maybe having a house with more yard space and less density of neighbors with dozens of kids. As time passed, we continued to think about another move. The housing market was not good, but we listed our house with a real estate agency. In the meantime, a house came up for sale just outside the Tuscumbia city limits. It was owned by Sonny and Jody Morris, who were building a new house in Florence, closer to his car dealership. The house was located on a dead-end street with seven houses on one side of the street, and a pasture across from them. The houses also had a field behind them. The lots were big and we thought this would be an excellent place to raise our children. They would attend school about three miles away at Colbert Heights. The Muscle Shoals house was only three or four miles away, so we drove over and looked at the house. It looked nice on the outside and had a one-acre lot. The house was built in the late '50s and did not have some of the modern conveniences of our house in Muscle Shoals. It had lots of room, with two baths and a full basement. After looking at the house, the owner of the realty company called to ask how we liked it. Barbara said there was no way we would buy that house, she didn't like the inside and it would require a lot of work to fix it up. We didn't give the house further consideration; however, Mr. Woody Walker called us again in a few days with a very attractive offer and asked if we would reconsider. We thought it was a good deal but there was a problem. The Morris family could not move until their new house was finished, and we had to sell our house. We wanted the Morris family to move out to allow us the chance to paint and do other work on the inside before we moved in. So, with the understanding that they would move as soon as possible, we closed the deal on the house hoping they would move out soon and we could sell our house in Muscle Shoals soon. As it worked out, neither of these things happened for over three months and we were stuck with two houses during that time.

We moved into 119 Tremont Drive in November 1968 after transferring our 5% FHA mortgage on the Muscle Shoals house to a friend at Ford. Julie was now 10 years old and Mike was eight, with little Roger three. Julie and Mike would attend school at Colbert Heights, which had grades 1 through 12 in the same complex and was operated by the Colbert County School System. The school bus came by our house, but after a few months we decided it was better to take them to school ourselves rather than ride the long route on the bus.

My part-time antenna business continued to increase every year. I felt myself becoming less interested in my job at Ford because it was not challenging any more. My job was one almost any young man would love to have, but my future was already determined if I worked there for the rest of my life. However, owning a business is very risky and entails great responsibility, especially when employees are involved. The challenge of trying to be successful is the strongest draw for one to be in business for themselves.

The house on Tremont Drive required more attention because there were so many things that needed to be upgraded. I had a project going just about all the time. Over the 30 years we lived there, we made numerous improvements to the house. We remodeled the kitchen twice, replaced all the windows, and installed a new central heating and air-conditioning system. We also painted the brick, added a front porch, a covered patio for the back, a new roof, new floors, and a driveway. The full basement was partitioned into rooms using half of the floor space for a bedroom, game room, bathroom, and an office. The other half was used as storage.

The one-acre yard required a lot of work in keeping the grass mowed. We purchased a riding lawnmower after the first year, which made it easier. The front portion of the yard was steeply sloped and caution was necessary while riding the mower for fear of it overturning. The back yard of the lot was extremely flat and level. It made a perfect place to play any type of sports.

On a few occasions while I cut the grass Mike asked to drive the mower. I let him sit on my lap and steer the small tractor mower around the yard a few times. Then later, when I was right there with him, he operated the mower by himself, going slow and carefully. Although he was only 11 at the time, he did a good job driving the mower, cutting the grass for a brief period of time while I watched close by. Mike was never allowed to operate the mower without me being with him. Being a kid at heart, I knew driving the mower was fun for the boys so I even let Roger steer the tractor while sitting on my lap sometimes. I shudder to think about the few times that Roger rode on the hood of the mower while I drove. This was such a foolish thing for a parent to do, and I should have known better.

My longtime friend, Bobby Henry, worked at Ford and was one of the best people who ever worked with me in the antenna business. Bob was very talented and could do almost anything. He had good judgment about things and was an all around good person. I loved to work with him and learn from him. One spring day, we had gone to Savannah, Tennessee, about 45 miles northwest, to work on an antenna which was mounted on a 100 foot tower. It was a bright, clear sunny day to be outside. We finished the job just after noon and were driving back. I had a two-way radio in my truck and a unit at home so Barbara and I could communicate if needed. About halfway back from Savannah the radio came on with someone trying to give me a message, but the signal was very weak and it was not intelligible. I knew it was not Barbara, but it had to be coming from my house. Then another transmission began and it was a man's voice saying, "Bobby, if you can hear me, come home." This frightened me a lot. I tried to talk back to the person who turned out to be my neighbor on Tremont Drive, R.N. McMackin. I asked him what was wrong and he said, "It's Roger, he's hurt." I thought he may have broken an arm or something, but when he said he was hurt badly by the lawnmower, I could hardly drive. I was extremely worried.

CHAPTER TEN

After receiving the shocking news about the accident, we raced down the highway toward home. The radio transmission became clearer as we grew closer. I was able to learn more about what had happened. I was told Roger would be taken to Huntsville and that he had been run over by the lawnmower. At this point I became so upset Bob told me to pull over and let him drive. We were told Barbara was at Dr. John Mims' office in Tuscumbia and to come there.

The first thing I thought was we needed to get to Huntsville fast, so I asked them to call the airport to ask if Ralph Montgomery could fly us to Huntsville. Ralph was co-owner of Muscle Shoals Aviation and had airplanes that they used for charter. I knew if Roger was being taken to Huntsville, he must be seriously injured. Meanwhile, with Bob Henry driving and speeding toward Tuscumbia, we arrived at the doctor's office within about 30 minutes.

When the accident happened, Barbara had reluctantly agreed for Mike to use the mower while she sat on the back patio watching him. In the meantime, the phone rang and she went inside the house to answer. In a very short time, as she looked through the kitchen window, she heard the mower stop and Mike screaming. She ran to the yard and saw Roger's legs and feet, but his body was under the mower. Barbara was in total shock and lifted the mower up while she and Mike pulled him from beneath it. She thought he was dead, and carried him into the house. The next door neighbor,

Evelyn Craig, came over to find out what had happened. They noticed that Roger was alive and she drove the car while Barbara and Mike held Roger in the back seat. Our daughter Julie was visiting her grandparents at the time. Mrs. Craig suggested they stop at Dr. Mims' office, which was the first possible place to receive medical care.

The hospital was in Sheffield, a few miles away, and at that time did not have a full-time doctor in the emergency room. It was a blessing they stopped at the doctor's office because they carried him in the side door and Dr. Mims was right there. Dr. John Mims was one of the most prominent doctors in the area, so I feel God directed the neighbor's actions. The doctor immediately assessed Roger's injuries and called the local funeral home to provide an ambulance to transport him to Huntsville Hospital, which is about 75 miles away. The area still did not have emergency response personnel and equipment. The doctor knew Roger needed a neuro-surgeon in order to have any possibility of survival. He was sliced through his brain down from the top of his head, through his face and mouth. A large portion of the skull bone was torn away, and he had a large cut down his midsection.

When I arrived at the doctor's office I saw Barbara covered with blood and crying, "Don't let my baby die."

Dr. Mims had already left with Roger in the ambulance for Huntsville. He left his office full of patients and rode with Roger all the way, administering an I.V. and doing all he could to control the bleeding. The highway to Huntsville was two-lane at that time, but the Tuscumbia police gave them an escort and called ahead for the towns on the route to expect them soon. Dr. Mims' office called Huntsville Hospital and alerted them regarding the incoming emergency. The hospital contacted the appropriate doctors and they were standing by waiting for his arrival.

Shortly after Bob Henry and I arrived at the doctor's office, Barbara and I were carried to the airport by my brother Johnny and my sister Vera, who by then were at the doctor's office. When we arrived at the Huntsville Airport, a police car was waiting and carried us to the hospital. The coordination of this event was unbelievable. All the way from Tuscumbia to the hospital Barbara and I cried and prayed that our little boy would be all right.

Roger, being the baby and so sweet and perfect, was special to me, not because I loved him more than the other two children, but he being born on my birthday and my growing up myself, gave me a better appreciation of having children. When we reached Huntsville Hospital Emergency Room, Dr. Mims was there in the waiting room. He was so nice and talked with us about Roger, saying that he was sometimes conscious and trying to tell him his name on the way from Tuscumbia. We could tell Dr. Mims was very concerned but didn't want to show it because we were already upset ourselves.

By that time, the word about the accident had spread all around the Shoals area and some of our close friends came to the hospital to support us. Our dear friends, Wayne and Sharon Green, and Ralph and Janell Montgomery, were among the first to come that night. It seemed like we waited for hours to get an update about Roger. Dr. Mims returned home with the ambulance and wished us well. We were very thankful for his kindness and dedication to come with Roger and care for him. Without his help Roger would have not made it through this ordeal.

We were not allowed to see Roger at all until the next day, but the doctors came out to talk to us after the long surgery. We hung on to every word they said as we struggled to control our emotions. They told us he might not live through the night, and it was going to be a slim chance for him to recover. I asked if Roger would be all right if he did recover from the brain injury, and the doctor said he believed he would be a vegetable if he lived.

At that point I thought our lives were over. I could not believe this was happening to us. In my mind I said, "Now God can fix this, and He's just going to have to do it." Then, while a few of our friends sat with Barbara, Wayne and Ralph took me walking on the sidewalk outside the hospital. The words of the doctor kept sounding in my ears and I could not accept their projections for our little boy's well-being. Wayne and Ralph did their best to console me, but my emotions were almost uncontrollable.

We all sat through the night, waiting for word from Roger. They told us that if he made it through the night we could see him in the morning. All through the night we prayed to God and asked Him to help us. I made up my mind that God was going to hear from me, and I was going to ask everyone to pray for my son's recovery.

The next morning, at 8:00 a.m., I called the newspaper in Florence and told them I wanted to run an ad in the paper. I already had an account with them through my antenna business. The lady asked me what I wanted the ad to say and I said "Just say, Pray for Roger Denton." The small ad ran the next day and the churches and people all over the Shoals area began praying for Roger. The newspaper ran a news story about the accident and a lot of attention was given to Roger's condition.

Later that morning, as we sat in the waiting room of the Intensive Care Unit, one of the doctors came out and said we could go in to see Roger for just a minute. He said, "I don't know if he can hear you or will know who you are, but please try not to show your emotions. If he can hear you crying or being emotional, that may upset him more." His head was completely bandaged and only one eye was not covered with the bandage, and it was swollen shut. Barbara and I slowly entered the quiet room and held each other as we stood by his bed and looked at him. Then I took his little hand into mine and said, "Roger, this is Daddy, if you can hear me squeeze my hand." He began squeezing my finger over and over again. We were so happy and I felt that God was going to help us. We stayed a few minutes, talking to him and encouraging him, saying he would be OK and that we loved him. We were allowed to see him again that night and were hopeful he would recover. We went to the hospital chapel to pray several times that day and through the days that followed.

As the days went by we began to have more hope, and were visited by numerous friends from home. The Tuscumbia Church of Christ, where we were members, offered up constant prayers for Roger, as did all the other churches in the area back home. One of the elders from our church, R.N. McMackin, and his son Mike, were frequent visitors and gave us great support. Over the years Mike McMackin has been a very true friend of our family. He is now an elder at the Tuscumbia Church.

As the days and weeks passed, Roger made steady progress and surprised the doctors with his recovery. When the day came for him to be transferred from the ICU into a room, we felt confident regarding his recovery. We both stayed in his room around the clock, sleeping briefly, using a hospital chair and a small cot.

I was lucky having my job at Ford because the company allowed me to take leave time while I was away in Huntsville. We worried about Julie and Mike not being with us, but we knew they would be fine staying with Barbara's parents in Sheffield. This shocking event took a huge toll on Barbara's Mom and Dad with them worried about Roger and us, along with caring for the two other grandchildren, Mike and Julie.

Within a few weeks we brought Roger home. We were so humbled and thankful for our prayers being answered. Roger had a turban-looking bandage covering his head. It had to be changed each day after we left the hospital, but Barbara had watched the nurses do it many times, so she performed that duty every day for the next few years as Roger went through several related operations to replace the missing skull and complications that followed.

After the neurosurgeon was satisfied with the brain repair, most of the remaining work was done by a plastic surgeon, who did a remarkable job. Without going into lengthy and graphic details, Roger was a miracle who God saved for a special purpose. He went to school his first year using a special speaker phone hookup with his classroom. Roger could hear the class proceedings and could answer questions from the teacher by pressing a button on the speaker box. This worked well and he felt a part of being in school. Because of further surgery, he attended school wearing his head bandage the next year without any trouble. He was not intimidated by his looks, and the other children loved him and were never hostile towards him.

My part-time business continued to grow. I had a very good location on a busy highway coming into Muscle Shoals, and had two full-time employees. As Roger improved to the point of being completely well, I began thinking about leaving my job at Ford and being full-time with my business. Later, I took a six-week leave of absence from Ford to test out my idea of being in business full-time. At the end of the six weeks we decided this was what I should do, and I resigned in the fall of 1971 after working for Ford 11 years and 10 months. I understood that I was leaving a very good job with excellent benefits and security; however, the desire to have my own business, and a chance to make a better life, was a powerful force in my mind.

Thinking Roger was well, and that situation was behind us, I devoted all my energy to making a go of the business. I later took on more employees and branched out into the retail side of the T.V. business, being a dealer for three major brands of T.V. sets.

One day Barbara asked me to look at Roger's forehead and see if I thought it was all right. His forehead was discolored and puffy where the doctors had replaced his missing skull with a man-made substance. His head had looked very good after the procedure, and we thought it was fine. But something was now wrong. We called the doctor in Huntsville and he recommended bringing him to see him as soon as possible. We carried Roger back to Huntsville and the doctor said his body had rejected the material and it would have to be removed. This was devastating to us because we didn't want to go through this situation again, but we had no choice. The surgery required removing the plastic-like material from a large portion of his forehead and later replacing it with two of his ribs grafted into place. With several subsequent operations necessary to finish this procedure, it was very trying on us, especially Roger, but he continued to be brave.

During the coming years, we did our best to raise the children while struggling to make ends meet with the little business. I was never a good manager of money, and would purchase new trucks and equipment for the business in order to do the job better and offer better service to the customers.

While I was away on a business trip to Burlington, Iowa, Barbara's Dad passed away suddenly. Eugene was the finest man I had ever known and was so good to me and my family. He never had a lot of material possessions, but he had a life record of kindness and love for everyone. When contacted by his sister, Peggy Simpson, to tell me the news, I could not believe it. I got a plane home, landing in Memphis, which was as close as I could get that night. Wayne Green and my brother-in-law, Winston Nash, came to Memphis and picked me up at the airport. It was sub-freezing weather for the long trip back to Sheffield. Eugene P. Jeffreys will always be remembered as a good man who loved others.

CHAPTER ELEVEN

After the death of Barbara's Dad, her mother had no income at all. Most people never realize the problems a widow has without experiencing it first hand. Eugene was 52 years old and Myrtie Lee was 50. He only had enough insurance to cover the funeral and related expenses. She did not qualify for social security or other benefits at her age. She was not allowed to draw from his social security before she became 62, which meant that unless she worked, she would have no income or health benefits for the next 12 years. She managed to get a job paying minimum wage, but had no health insurance. Medicare is only available for people 65 and older.

By then, I needed someone to answer the phone and look after the office. Although Myrtie Lee had no experience and limited office skills, she went to work for Bobby Denton Company. We were able to pay her a little more and provide the company Blue Cross insurance coverage. She was a very conscientious employee and everyone loved having her with us. The boys who worked for me called her Mamaw, as did the grandchildren. That became her name to all of us.

The next few years were fairly normal for the family. Our then teenage daughter Julie was a cheerleader at the high school. We attended all the games, both football and basketball, to support her. I didn't realize then how beautiful it was to come home and see the cheerleaders practicing in the backyard and the boys,

Mike and Roger, shooting basketball in the paved parking area in the back.

We went through most of the usual family things, like camping and going to the lake where my brother had a lakeside house. Camping was popular then and most of our friends, like Gerald and Betty Aker, and Wayne and Sharon Green, had travel trailers or some kind of camping equipment to pull for a weekend at a campground within the region. We had a good time and the kids all loved it, cooking out and making ice-cream or just sitting by a campfire talking. Bob and Mary Alice Henry would always make the ice-cream.

When Mike was 15-years old, we bought him a new bicycle. Tremont Drive was a dead-end street about a quarter of a mile long. It was a good street for the kids to ride but they had strict instructions not to go beyond our street on to Woodmont Drive, which was the county road going to Colbert Heights. One day Mike asked if he could ride his bicycle to the store located on Woodmont Drive. I had refused to allow him to go several times before. But, after thinking about it and knowing the store was only a short distance down the road, I said yes, with instructions to watch out for the traffic and be careful. Mike was a strong, experienced rider. I thought it was fine for him to go on the short trip to the store. It would be fun for him.

After Mike had been gone for several minutes, the lady who lived at the corner of Woodmont Drive and Tremont Drive came to the house and said, "Come quickly, Mike has been hit by a car." We jumped into the car and rushed up the road. As we came near the site, we saw lots of cars parked on the side of the road. A friend of mine, Sam Meadows, came and met our car and said Barbara, Julie and Roger should stay in the car while I went to see about Mike. They wanted to go see about him also, but it would not have been good for them to see him at that time. I had no idea what to expect as I ran up the road. I saw a car off the road, sitting in the edge of a field. When I got to the location, Mike and his bicycle were crumpled and lying behind the car. He was conscious. As I approached him I said, "Son, I am so sorry. We are being tested again." Mike was very brave. I could see that his legs were broken and he was in terrible pain. Because he and the bicycle were at the back of the car, it was clear that the car had hit him on the road and rolled him beneath it, through a fence and into the field. By that time an ambulance arrived with the police. This time it was a real ambulance, not a funeral home hearse I had experienced before. Colbert County Hospital had purchased the vehicle just a short time before to serve their emergency room. I asked Sam to go to my car and tell Barbara and the kids that Mike was going to the hospital and I was riding with him. The ambulance had two paramedics who were careful and did all they could for him as we made the trip to the hospital. We went up Woodmont Drive going right past Dr. Mims' office where Roger was taken about six years before.

Mike was taken into the emergency room and treated. He was later sent to ICU where he stayed several days. He was critically injured, with 15 broken bones and internal injuries. The person driving the car was a teacher at Colbert Heights School. She was traveling in the same direction as Mike when the car hit him. We felt sorry for the lady because we knew she would not have done this on purpose. Mike had several surgeries over the next several days and was placed in traction while he recovered. He endured this situation well and we gave him all our support, as he spent 99 days in the hospital before coming home. He was determined not to let his injuries keep him down. He played shooting basketball while on crutches. He used the crutches several weeks after being dismissed from the hospital.

With these horrific events occurring in our lives, I wondered if I was being punished for some reason. I didn't understand why we were having so much trouble when others may not experience near as much in their entire lifetime. But, I thought how lucky we had been to come through these tragedies and still have our children. I believe everyone reacts differently in dealing with despair as well as prosperity. Some cannot handle power or financial success or adversity. Some people turn away from God, and some turn towards Him.

Our faith is all we have when we are convinced that a situation is beyond our control. Only our faith can give us the peace of mind needed to cope with serious problems. We do not have to look far to find people who have problems worse than ours. I know it is easy to say, but I truly believe that a person who has faith in God can endure troubles and adversity much better than those who do not know God. However, we can still have extreme problems in our lives, even though we have faith in God. I have had people tell me many times that the Bible says God will not allow us to suffer beyond that which we can bear. That's not what it says. What about the Christians who were fed to the lions, and the many other references regarding Christians being put to death because of their faith? Consider the story of Job in the Bible. He lost everything he had but refused to blame God. The scripture these people are referring to is I Corinthians 10:13, and is clearly talking about temptation. The scripture says that God will not allow you to be tempted beyond your strength, and will provide a way of escape that you may be able to endure it. When the rain comes, it rains on the bad man's farm just as it does on the good man's farm.

Julie began driving after she was 16. We bought her a new little Chevrolet car that she loved so much. She drove it for years until it was worn completely out. Then Mike was next to get a car. He wanted a sportier car, so we got him a new Pontiac Firebird which only cost about $5,000 at that time. While they were learning to drive, I tried to teach them some of the things they might experience while driving. One of the most important things was that of running off the pavement. If they ever felt that experience and quickly over steered the car back on to the road, they could have a bad accident. That is one of the most common causes of teenage accidents.

It is a great learning experience raising two teenagers at the same time. One day, after discussing some do's and don'ts with them, they said to me, "Daddy, you just don't understand," and I said, "You're right, I don't, because I have never been a Daddy of teenagers before and you have never been a teenager before, so we will have to learn how to do this together."

When Mike only had his new car for a few weeks, we were all going to church for Wednesday night Bible study, and Mike left early to go pick up his friend Raymond to go with him. Within a few minutes, as we were about to leave the house, the phone range and it was Mike. He said, "Daddy, you're not going to believe this, but I have just hit a kid down here on Frankfort Road." He was right; I could hardly believe it. We rushed to the scene and found Mike's car sitting on the street and a big, healthy boy about 12 years old laying in a yard on the other side of the street. We quickly went over to check on him, and his mother was giving him a strong talking to about crossing the street and not being careful. He was in pain, but his only injury was a broken leg which was bad, but we were thankful it was not worse. He and the witnesses said that as he was about to run across the street he looked and saw a car and waited for it, then ran out after it passed and could not see Mike's car right behind the other one. They said it was unavoidable and there was no speeding involved. Our insurance company paid his hospital and doctor bills. We visited him every day for several days.

Julie had been in love with number 6, Philip McCreary, on the Colbert Heights football team for years. She graduated from high school and didn't want to go to college. She went to work at a local bank and was very happy. Until she was married, she stayed close and always came home from dates with Philip by curfew time. Julie and Philip were a committed young couple and never dated anyone else.

Although Mike had problems with his legs and knees as a result of his accident, he insisted on playing football. He was number 74, a big healthy kid, and did a good job playing right tackle for the Colbert Heights Wildcats. As we watched the games we always sat in fear that he'd be injured. He was a few times, but never seriously.

Roger continued to do well, and was growing up as smart as a whip, and making good grades in school. His favorite pastime was riding his go-cart on his little race track out back at the edge of the field. Another fun thing for him was playing TV preacher with his friend Steve Clark, the son of our friends Charles and Betty Clark.

They would set up their little ministry in the basement and imitate the charismatic preachers on TV. I guess they wanted to exhibit the extreme because our church was so conservative. Of course, they were playing in private and would never do that in a public setting.

We did a lot of things with Charles and Betty. They owned the Kentucky Fried Chicken franchise in the area. One trip we made together was to Little Rock to meet a former preacher of the church in Tuscumbia, and his wife. Hal and Aletta Smith had been our close friends and moved to Texas the year before. We all traveled to Little Rock to spend the weekend because it was about half-way for each of us. Charles and Betty rode with us in our car. They drove over to our house, and we loaded up the luggage and left for Little Rock. When we arrived at the hotel and began unloading the luggage, Barbara and I had failed to load our luggage in the trunk and had left it at home. We didn't have a thing for the weekend stay. We called home immediately and Julie said, "You left your luggage here and I've already gone to the bus station and shipped it to you." We were so proud of her for such quick thinking. We went to the bus station the next morning and picked up our luggage. The visit with Hal and Aletta was nice, and we all had a real good time together. Although Hal and Aletta have moved a few times since then, they continue to live in North Texas, and after more than 30 years, we all continue to be good friends. Charles and Betty have turned their business over to the children and are enjoying semi-retirement.

As I became older and more mature, my thoughts became attracted to community service and government. I can't explain why one wants to serve as an elected official, but I just felt drawn to give it a try. At first, I thought about the county school board, but decided that I would be more suited serving as a member of the Colbert County Commission. It was a part-time job and only paid $250 per month at that time. I looked into the possibility and was sure that my name recognition was good because of my music and business background. After the experience of having no full-time doctor in the emergency room at the Colbert County Hospital, I made this my number one issue and promised to get that done if elected. My opponent was B.D. Kimbrough, an old friend and a good person who was running for another term. I didn't know about any of the old-school politics but just got out there and was myself, asking people to vote for me. As it turned out, B.D. and I were the only candidates running in that district, so that meant there would be no run-off after the primary, and no opposition in the general election later that November.

I was 38 years old, and B.D. was about 10 years older. He certainly had more experience and knowledge about government, but after all these years of elected service, I have determined that it's all about if people like you and trust you.

CHAPTER TWELVE

After being elected to the Colbert County Commission in the spring of 1976, I was humbled by the public's trust in me. I began reading the paper and listening to local news more to be aware of things going on in the county. It seemed like forever from the time I was elected in the spring, until the time to take office in mid-January. By the time I officially took office, my main campaign promise was already fulfilled. Because of my campaign regarding a full-time doctor at the emergency room, the Hospital Board agreed to put in place a program partnering with UAB, the University of Alabama in Birmingham. This service would be provided through the Medical School by sending intern doctors in training to the Colbert County Hospital on a rotating basis for a few days at a time. This program worked well for several years.

It was exciting for me serving on the Colbert County Commission. The challenges were many and I wanted to bring a more progressive element to the governing body of the county. The county was completely debt free, which was very unusual for the 67 counties in Alabama. In years past, there had been serious financial mismanagement.

The county elected officials were determined not to allow this to happen again. For the past 20 years, before I was elected, the county managed to pay off all its debts and save enough to pay cash for a new wing on the courthouse, complete with all new furnishings. The biggest reason for the county's financial problems was its road department. Each of the four commissioners was full-time and operated their own road department within the district. So, instead of having a county road department, we had four road departments. Each department had its own equipment and employees. This condition still exists in many counties throughout Alabama today.

This style of county road management caused Colbert County and several other counties to have their road departments placed into receivership of the State Highway Department. The situation was called "Captive Counties" and was completcly managed by the State Highway Department. The State took all the counties' equipment and the funds that were dedicated for building and maintaining its roads. These funds were placed in an account for operating the road system in that county.

Thanks to the leadership of newly elected Governor Fob James and the new legislature elected in 1978, this practice of Captive Counties was stopped. Although the action was very controversial, it was the right thing to do. The counties of Alabama should operate their own road departments without state control.

One of the best things that our local legislative delegation has done for the citizens of our counties of Northwest Alabama was to pass legislation creating a "Unit System" for each county. The unit system meant the County Commission would administer one road department in the county, with a professional engineer overseeing it. Some of the citizens were skeptical about the change. They thought that it might result in the county going back to the same old inefficient way of running the road department; however, this was not the case. All the counties that have changed over to the unit system have prospered. The counties around the state that continue to use the old district road system are, for the most part, deeply in debt.

My two years as a member of the Colbert County Commission were very good for me. Times and technology were changing. A lot of things needed to be done to keep up with the public needs. Colbert County was one of the first counties in the state to purchase a computer system. Dozens of counties throughout Alabama purchased the program from Colbert County to implement in their tax collection system.

There were several other things that were accomplished during that time. We constructed a new modern Health Department building and initiated a large county water system serving most portions of the rural area.

I continued to operate my antenna business which became the largest antenna dealer in the southeast. We expanded into more commercial work for Motorola and General Electric two-way radio system towers, AM and FM radio station towers, and athletic playing field lighting towers. With all I had going on, one would think I would not be thinking about further involvement in politics.

I love people and the pleasure of serving them in a public service capacity. During that time, my good friend Ronnie Flippo was our state senator in Alabama and was elected to Congress to serve the Fifth Congressional District, which composed seven counties across North Alabama. To fill Ronnie's seat as state senator, the Alabama Constitution stipulates a special election must be held for the selection of his replacement. A local Democrat Party candidate, Jimmy Hunt, qualified to run and was the only candidate to be on the special election ballot. There was some discontentment because people wanted to have a choice and Oscar Ray Peden of Florence qualified to run as an Independent.

As the special election drew near, the campaign became heated. The Senate District 1, one of the 35 districts in the state, was composed of Lauderdale County, most of the population of Colbert County, and the extreme western portion of Franklin County. Jimmy Hunt was a well-known attorney in Tuscumbia, and Oscar Ray Peden was a very outspoken and well-known member of the Florence City Commission. Oscar Ray won the race and went directly to Montgomery to be sworn in, and began serving because the Legislature was in session at that time. He soon became known as the senator from North Alabama who loved to filibuster the issues.

I became interested in politics at the state level and soon began to think that I would like to serve as senator for Northwest Alabama. The term I was serving as County Commissioner was not ending for two years after the senate position expired, so if I were to run for the senate and didn't win, I would continue serving as County Commissioner for two more years. When I mentioned the possibility of running to others, some would say, "it's a very big district and would require a lot of money and hard work." However, in my mind I knew I was very well-known throughout the district and would do well.

A Senate District is made up of 3 House of Representative Districts and consists of about 150,000 people. Senate District 1 had two House seats in Lauderdale County and one consisting of parts of Colbert and Franklin Counties at that time. The old time politicians thought since most of the voters were in Lauderdale County, a candidate who lived in Colbert County could not win.

Somehow, I felt that I was being drawn to run and that this was something God had planned for me to do. The other candidate in the race was Bob Hill from Florence. He was a 12-year veteran of the House of Representatives and had good name recognition. His Dad had been a very popular judge in Lauderdale County and Bob was an astute attorney who had experience in the legislative process. The feeling of the so-called political experts was that Oscar Ray needed to be replaced, but they thought Bob would be the candidate who would win. I was not knowledgeable in high-rolling politics and didn't know much about the legislative process. I didn't know about Special Interest Groups who were interested in working for or against a candidate. I just believed what I believed and hoped the voters would choose me.

My only funding came from individuals and small businesses around the area and one large group who had never taken an active part in supporting a candidate for the State Senate before. They were the Alabama Farm Bureau, that later became ALFA. They gave me about $8,000 and provided technical help and assistance, along with a person to help me in the campaign. When the primary election was over, I received the most votes of the three candidates, and spent the least amount of money. A run-off would be held between Oscar Ray and me in about three weeks. That was the hardest part, but I won the final race and we all were very happy.

George Wallace was the Governor, and Fob James was just elected to take his place in January. But, I, being a newly elected State Senator, took the new office immediately after being elected. Several of my friends and I requested that Governor Wallace appoint our friend Charles Thompson to fill my unexpired term as County Commissioner, and he did. Charles went on to be re-elected and then to serve as Chairman of the Commission for several years.

The next year I made one of the biggest mistakes I had ever made. I expanded my business by buying a building and property at a new location. The timing could not have been worse. It was the beginning of the '80s and Ronald Reagan had just taken office. The economic recession came and interest rates went as high as 22% for business loans. I struggled hard to make the situation work out, but with being gone three days a week, the business suffered. I knew that another life-changing decision would have to be made. I was going broke fast, and I knew it was going to be over soon. Another big dream that I had nurtured for most of my life was going to come to an end.

The choices I had were to go bankrupt, or liquidate the inventory, equipment and property, and try to pay off the balance when I could find another job. Although I later thought it might have been better to have used the bankruptcy law and gotten away clean and free of residual debt, this was just not the way I was raised. I wanted to make sure that all my remaining debts were paid in full. So, when the decision was made to liquidate and close the business, I felt somewhat relieved and set out to make the best of it. One of the first things I did was to spread the word around that I was looking for a job and going out of business.

Later, Ed Mauldin, a long-time friend and founder of First Colbert Bank, contacted me regarding a job at the bank. I told him that all my experience with banks had been on the borrowing side of the desk. He said, "That's OK, we wouldn't need you to make loans; we need you to get new business for the bank." I had no idea what the job of Business Development Officer entailed.

After a few meetings with Mr. Mauldin, I accepted the job and was very thankful for the opportunity. I also worked hard to dispose of all the business assets and the large negative balance. Mr. Mauldin and the bank worked with me to structure a loan to cover it all. I paid back the loan over the next several years through monthly payments. I continue to have very fond memories of the people who had faith in me and helped me through this ordeal in my life.

I was employed as vice president at the bank, which later became Bank Independent, for five years. The bank experienced exceptional growth during the years I was with them, and continues to be one of the leading community banks in Alabama.

CHAPTER THIRTEEN

The '80s were filled with happy and sad times. My dear mother died after an extended illness, leaving my dad living alone in their little house in Cherokee.

Our daughter Julie married Philip in a nice wedding at the Church of Christ in Tuscumbia. I was very proud of them after so many years of being devoted to each other. Julie had often said that all she ever wanted to be was a wife and a mother. Although she has proven to be an excellent wife, she was never able to have children. I am convinced that God had other plans, and has allowed her to be the loving and caring angel she has always been to others.

Later, our son Mike married Lynne Fuller of Muscle Shoals. They gave us our first grandson, Matthew, and then a granddaughter, Ashley.

Our youngest son, Roger, married Devona Pounders of the Hawk Pride community, and they had our third grandchild, Jordan. As all grandparents, we were filled with joy seeing the grandchildren grow and be a part of our lives. We are very proud of them all, as they are proving themselves and developing their adult lives.

My work in the State Senate was very involved as I served on numerous committees. Because of the early '80s recession, the economic condition of the Shoals was devastated. This area needed several things done to transition and be more diverse in employment. Over the years, several large industries were providing thousands of good paying jobs, but the area had not looked beyond that time of prosperity to prepare for the future.

I have chosen not to indulge in this writing the extent of my involvement regarding the changes which have occurred over the more than 30 years serving as the State Senator for the Shoals area. I have always thought political leaders should not brag on themselves and take credit for what the people elected them to do, but after they are gone, should they be due credit for things they have accomplished, that would be more proper.

When I entered the political arena, I never in my wildest dreams thought that I, as a poor sharecropper's son, would be elected to be a member of the State Senate, and to be the longest continuous serving member of that august institution. All those years I spent believing that everyone was smarter than I because I didn't make good grades in school and never went to college until I was a grandfather, kept me humble while going about my duties in government.

After all these years dealing with the highest levels of elected officials, I have decided that many of them are not as smart as they think they are, and may even be a legend in their own mind. We always think that the people making the decisions in Washington and in our state know what they are doing. The sad thing is, sometimes they don't. However, for the most part, most people serving us in government are good, and smart, well-meaning individuals who want to do the right things.

My job at the bank was good for me and allowed me to do the political part-time job with flexibility. I represented the bank in several ways other than just soliciting new account business. I remembered reading about a branch bank being located inside a Kroger store in another state. It came to mind when the news came that Florence would be getting a new Kroger store on the fast developing eastern side of town. So, I thought this could be a location suited for a new branch. After contacting the Kroger Company and visiting their corporate office, one of Mr. Mauldin's sons, who was an officer at the bank, and I flew to see the Kroger store with a bank inside. We interviewed the bank personnel and the manager of the store. I also made pictures, which we later used in our presentation to our bank officers and Board. It was decided to go forward with the project. When the new store opened, we had a new branch opening inside. It worked out well for several years until a new free-standing branch bank was built.

When I was employed with the bank just over five years, the local Junior College advertised for a new position of Director of Development. The college, Northwest Alabama State Junior College, had its main campus located in Phil Campbell, about 30 miles south of Muscle Shoals. The job would be for someone to oversee the development of a Foundation for the college, and also work towards the development of a satellite campus in Tuscumbia, which only had about 200 students. I applied for the position, which offered a better salary and benefits. I was interviewed by a committee at the college, and was recommended to the President, Charlie Britnell, for the job. The position was very challenging and I took it on with high hopes of success for the small college. I worked with a consultant from Santa Fe Community College in Gainesville, Florida, for two years. The studies with him were funded by a Federal grant. I studied foundation development and began establishing a Foundation for our college, which was a 501(c) 3 non-profit corporation. Within a year, we had a full slate of Board members for the Foundation. They were the top people in the college service area. Our purpose was to make the community aware of the college and what it had to offer. The ultimate goal was to raise large amounts of money to provide scholarships for the students and financial support for the college. This concept had never been done as an organized and professional effort and became very successful.

Over the years, the two-year colleges went through a transition of mergers and reorganization. The colleges were becoming more attractive to modern day students, who in years past did not give junior colleges around the state much thought. Through programs like we had at Northwest, the public began to slowly become attracted to the small college concept. Up until these years, the system did not have good credibility with the public. Published stories about kids taking classes at a junior college and then finding out that the credits would not transfer to a four-year college did considerable damage. The State School Board finally decided action needed to be taken to correct this problem. First of all, the two-year schools had been a step-child of our education system since they began. Under the early George Wallace administrations they were very political, being overseen by the elected State School Board.

With the leadership of Dr. Fred Gainus as Chancellor of the two-year system, all junior colleges began to offer only transferable courses and all the colleges were given a timeframe to become an accredited community college. This action, approved by the State School Board, began to change the image of these schools drastically. The Legislature took notice and began to fund the two-year colleges better.

The perfect example of the poor oversight of the colleges was here in the northwest portion of Alabama. We had a junior college with its main campus located in Phil Campbell, with a branch campus in Tuscumbia. The Tuscumbia campus was only two miles from a state technical college. Another technical college in Hamilton was just a few miles south of the Phil Campbell campus. It was the height of wasted duplication, but the communities didn't want to lose their colleges. After a few years of merging and re-arranging, the colleges were all settled into orderly institutions of education. The newly created community college offered both academic and technical courses. The tax payers have been given a much better return by this much needed change.

As I continued serving as the State Senator and as a college administrator, not having a formal college degree troubled me constantly. At my age, I did not expect to go for a higher position in politics or in my employment. I had a specialized profession at the college that one could not receive a degree for anyway. However, I wanted to have a degree to prove to myself that I could and to shed the feelings I had had from a kid in school.

Being a senator without being a college graduate, and being a college administrator without having a degree, was pulling heavily on my inner being. Although I have known several successful people who have made millions and didn't finish high school, I suppose I was just making a big to-do over nothing. But, I was determined to have an earned college degree.

After making contact with the University of Alabama, I was told about their distance learning degree program called "New College," which had been in place for several years. The program was considered the best distance learning program in the country. It received great accolades from the educational world. I went to Tuscaloosa for a two-day session and enrolled. I knew it wasn't going to be easy; they didn't give life experience credit and they didn't care if you were a senator or a janitor. The program had a reputation to live up to. This program was used more by students who only needed a few credits to graduate, or for those who dropped out of college and could not go full-time on a college campus. In my case, I had zero college credits and was an old guy starting from scratch. I worked on my studies every night and on weekends. I carried my work to Montgomery with me to study at night. At one point I almost quit after thinking "What are you doing this for? You won't get a raise if you finish, you won't be any more important, so why put yourself through all this work for years?" Then I thought, "because this is for me; I'm not trying to prove anything to anyone else."

My grades were so good, I almost began to like being in school. If only somehow I had gotten turned on to school as a kid I might have become something big. In May 1996, I walked across the stage at the University of Alabama in Tuscaloosa and received my Bachelor of Arts Degree with honors (Cum Laude). All my children and grandchildren were there and we had a real celebration. It was one of the happiest days of my life. Sometimes I still pinch myself to be sure it's me and if I really did it.

After receiving my college degree, I felt an inner peace and feeling of real accomplishment I had never felt before. It was just something about it that gave me confidence that I never had before. Not that I went around telling people about it, but just knowing myself that I had completed something that had troubled me most of my life. My wife, Barbara, who did not complain about my working on my studies at night and on weekends, is due a lot of credit. We missed out on many things because of my involvement in the college studies.

As I approach the final year of my eighth term as State Senator, I think back on the round-the-clock sessions and the trying round trips of over 400 miles each week, and wonder why I did it. This is one of the hardest questions to answer by a person who serves in politics. I'm sure there are several fancy replies that could be given regarding this question. It could be because of power or ego or other things; it is not money, for sure.

I have a good neighbor next door who asked me if I planned to seek another term of office. After telling him that I was not sure yet, he said, "Well, you'll have a real good retirement if you don't." That's what almost everyone in Alabama thinks, but the truth is a member of the Alabama State Legislature has no retirement or any other benefits for their service. Most people think we get what Congress receives, but we don't, no matter how long we may serve. I'm not complaining at all because it has been a major chapter in my life that I am very thankful for. To come from where I was born, and to do all the things I have done, it is a blessing and I humbly appreciate the trust the people have given me by allowing me to serve them. Now, after 32 years in the State Senate, and two years as a member of the Colbert County Commission, it's time for someone new to take the position. There are many good people who can do it well.

CHAPTER FOURTEEN

My Dad passed away in his sleep in 1991. He struggled for more than two years from small strokes which gradually affected his ability to talk. His walking and regular activities continued to be normal. But, over time he finally became unable to speak at all. He was 92 years old. He was a kind and happy man his entire life. His love for music was one of his greatest past-times. After my mother's death, Daddy lived alone in Cherokee for several years. As he grew older, the children all kept him at their homes at times. He soon became tired of living with others and said he would like to live at the nursing home where my mother had lived a few years before her death. He enjoyed being with people, laughing and talking with them. Daddy was a very well-liked resident at the nursing home and was happy until he died.

Daddy's funeral was somewhat unusual. At his request, one of his old friends, who played the banjo like he did, played the banjo at the funeral. It was a touching experience. Everyone knew that the old-time song that was played gave a perfect example of who he was. Along with the banjo tune, the funeral home played two songs that I had recorded a few years earlier, "Peace in the Valley" and "Just a Closer Walk with Thee." I had recorded the two gospel songs at Wishbone Studios in Muscle Shoals as a promotional project for the Alabama Music Hall of Fame. Terry Woodford owned the studio and produced dozens of hit records over the years.

The history of music in the Shoals area has deep roots, and the area has become famous all over the world from its' beginning by some kids who loved to play music. They had no idea that history was being made through their efforts, but the humble beginnings of a lot of people established the Muscle Shoals area as a great music icon in the world. There are numerous stories that can be written regarding the several recording studios and the dozens of people who have made the music of the Shoals what it was and still is today.

Soon after I was elected to the State Senate in 1978, a few of my old friends in the music business around the area met with me to talk about the possibility of establishing an Alabama Music Hall of Fame and locating it in the Muscle Shoals area. We decided to try and pass legislation for its creation with the special stipulations that the Board would be appointed from all over the state, but the majority of the Board members would have to live in the general area of The Shoals to ensure that meetings could be held with a quorum present. State Representatives Tom Coburn from Tuscumbia, Joe Goodwin of Muscle Shoals, and Nelson Starkey of Florence, were all very involved with the effort. The Bill was passed through the Legislature and became law. So then we had a Hall of Fame, but it was only a Board to be appointed by the Governor. The Legislature did not provide funding for the operations or a building. All that came after years of hard work and political struggles. As I think back over all the things that have been accomplished regarding the Alabama Music Hall of Fame, the person whom I believe worked the dream the hardest and had the determination to see this project a reality, was the first executive director, Lola Scobey. Throughout the early years she worked with no funding and very little help to get a thankless job done. Others have worked hard also, but Lola was my champion. The first president of the Board, Terry Woodford, along with Jimmy Durham, Jimmy Johnson, Rick Hall, David Johnson, James Joiner and many others, played a huge role in seeing this mammoth project completed.

The Alabama Music Hall of Fame is a fine museum projecting all the people in our state who made a contribution to our musical heritage. Through the ensuing years, a state bond issue provided the funds to build a nice, new building located on Highway 72 in Tuscumbia. It has functioned well over the years with very limited funding other than admission ticket sales and small fund raisers. The state has provided funds over the years, but the funds for the arts and museums have never been a high priority by most governors and legislators. A few years after the building was completed, some of the Board members asked the Governor to appoint me as a member of the Board of Directors. It was a high honor for me to serve. The terms were for six years, but members could have the possibility of being reappointed for future terms. I have always thought the Board should not be political, but it has always been that way.

With each new governor, new Board members were appointed in most cases. On the last day of former Governor Fob James' term, he replaced me as a member of the Board, and the same thing happened to Board member James Joiner after a new governor took office a few years before. I have spoken with the Board members in the past regarding my idea of allowing a different selection process for the membership, but they did not want a change to be made. I believe the Board members should have a burning desire to work hard in an unselfish manner to promote the institution. The present members are very good people, but one should not have to be politically connected in order to be appointed to the Board.

One day, while talking with my good friends Jimmy Johnson and the late Ava Aldridge about music, the subject of my recording an album with the proceeds to go to the Hall of Fame came up. It was 1997, and I had not sung in years, but I said I would love to try to make a gospel album. I agreed to raise the money to pay for the expense if they would produce it as their contribution. They both quickly said yes, and the project was launched. Within a couple of months, we had a first-class gospel album of 13 old-time songs. Jimmy and Ava arranged to get the best musicians in the area to do the session. We cut the basic soundtracks at Rick Hall's FAME Studio in Muscle Shoals and did the vocals at Rain Tree Studio in Sheffield, owned by Lenny LeBlanc. We did most overdub recording at Muscle Shoals Sound Studio in Sheffield, which was operated by Roger Hawkins. The title of the CD is *My God and I,* and was distributed by Books-A-Million throughout the south. After the CD was released, I became more confident singing again after 40 years away from the business. I purchased a small sound system and began performing for small audiences around the area, singing with the soundtracks mostly to senior citizens. They loved the old-time gospel songs especially. In the meantime, Jimmy and Ava helped me cut a track of my first record that I made in the '50s, "A Fallen Star," so I sang it on the programs also. The CD sold well and raised money for the Hall of Fame. I just tell folks it did almost as well as all my other records, and sold less than a million. The next year I released a new gospel CD titled *HOPE*, and followed it with one called *Love Songs*, then another Alabama *Welcomes You*, and still another gospel album, *If There's Still Time*, which is my favorite. The next one was a collection of some of my original songs that I had recorded in the '50s *I Wish I was 18 Again.* Then my latest *Memories Are Made of This*, *Hooked on Music*, and *Rockin Old,* In addition to all these recordings, I have made three single CDs, *Love Can Build a Bridge*, *Now That You Know Where Heaven Is*, and *In the Arms of the Angels*.

The individuals who helped me record these songs will always be very special to me.

These recordings have given me great pleasure as a hobby that I love in my senior years. Oh yes, I can't pass up the opportunity to say all these CDs are available at www.bobbydenton.com.

Recording all these songs has been an experience that has come full circle. My first encounter in recording was very primitive. The industry later advanced to an analog system, which allowed track recording. The first analog studios did not consist of extra elaborate equipment; however, the more recent analog studios required hundreds of thousands of dollars for equipment and used magnetic recording tape, two-inches wide and running at speeds up to 30-inches per second. All these systems are considered dinosaurs in today's recording studios. They have been using a digital system for years, but digital has changed several times and is now computerized to a point of disbelief for we older people who have seen the transition occur over the last 50 years. After reflecting back on all the songs I have recorded, I am very proud of the opportunity to have one of my sons, and two of my grandsons be a part of my recordings. My son Roger sang with me on parts of the song "You Are My Sunshine," which is on the *Love Songs* album. My oldest grandson, Matt, played an electric guitar break on the song "You Were Always on My Mind," which is on the same album. My youngest grandson, Jordan, played acoustic guitar on the song "Go Rest High" for the album *Memories Are Made of This*, as well as both acoustic and electric guitar on my CD *Rockin' Old*. Having these members of my family be a part of my music in this last round of my music career has been very satisfying to me.

CHAPTER FIFTEEN

Our son Mike, who was badly injured in a car/bicycle accident when he was 15 years old, had grown up, married, and was the father of two wonderful children, Matt and Ashley. Mike worked at Champion Paper Company for several years. It was a good job and a very good company to work for. Over the years, Mike had a few problems with his left knee and leg as a result of his injury when he was young. He underwent treatment by an orthopedic doctor for a long time, and managed to continue to work at his job.

Due to a reduction in the workforce at the plant, Mike was transferred from his regular job in the lab to a job out in the plant, which required him to stand on his feet most of the time. This was not good for his ailing knee and it began to give him more trouble. The knee would swell and the pain was hard to bear. His orthopedic doctor suggested that he may need a knee replacement, and Mike took it under consideration. He talked with us about making the decision and I suggested he go to Birmingham to the Sports Medicine Clinic for the surgery. He didn't like the idea of going to Birmingham and liked his doctor here in The Shoals. Mike was a big fan of the doctor because he had been a star football player at the University of Tennessee. Mike trusted him and felt more comfortable with him doing the replacement.

The procedure was done, and he went through a long recovery, with therapy, for several weeks. It seemed the knee was just not healing as it should, but like most men, he didn't always return to the doctor to complain as he should have. In the meantime, Mike and Lynn divorced after several years of drifting apart. This was very upsetting for all the family. Mike took it hard adjusting to a different life, living alone in an apartment in Tuscumbia. The children, as all children who are victims of divorce, were torn and struggled with the uncertain future.

As the months went by, Mike's knee was not doing well. It was red and swollen. We could tell something was wrong, but Mike continued to resist pursuing the problem. As he tried hard to maintain a normal lifestyle, the knee was always in his way. The company would not let him return to work unless he could do the job without restrictions. He applied for Social Security disability. After waiting for months, he was turned down. He reapplied and was turned down again. Luckily, he was able to maintain his medical insurance and received a small medical leave income from the company.

Mike loved his mother and grandmother especially. They talked several times every day. His grandmother, who was Barbara's mother, Myrtie Jeffreys, or Mamaw as we all called her, lived about a block away from Mike's apartment, and he would visit with her often. One day, Mike called Barbara and said, "Mama, I have something really wrong with my knee. I can't get out of bed." Barbara rushed over to see about him and immediately knew he had to see the doctor. His knee was blood-red and swollen very large. They went to see the doctor and he drew a large vial of liquid from the knee and said "Take him to the hospital immediately." The next day he told Mike his knee had an infection and the prosthetic would have to be removed. After checking into the Helen Keller Memorial Hospital, it was very clear that Mike had a very serious problem with his knee. The doctor later that day said it was a bad infection and they would do all they could to cure it. They removed the joint and began giving him massive amounts of antibiotics, trying to kill the infection. He lay helpless without a knee joint, with it heavily bandaged. The doctor consulted with the infectious disease specialist in Birmingham, and said he was doing all that could be done. Another week passed as we stood by him thinking somehow he would show improvement. But he didn't improve. We were very worried. The doctor finally arranged for him to be transferred to UAB in Birmingham. The hospital in Birmingham contemplated how he should be transported. They decided to send their ambulance with a nurse and doctor for him. After about two hours, the crew arrived and went in to see Mike to pre-medicate him for the trip. After they finished, and were about to leave for Birmingham, we went in to talk to Mike to assure him that we were coming right behind the ambulance. Mike said to me, "Daddy, I don't feel good about going to Birmingham." We only had a few brief moments, I asked him if he was OK with Jesus, and he said, "Yes." The trip to Birmingham was fast and scary, not knowing what the future held for our son.

As we went through the two weeks at the hospital at home, we heard the word "infection" dozens of times, but the words "staph infection" were never used by the doctors or nursing personnel. But that's what our son had and they knew it. They just didn't want to talk about it.

Staph infection is an infection caused by bacteria of the genus, staphylococcus, and there are more than 30 species. According to the Center for Disease Control and Prevention Health Care Association, infections account for an estimated 1.7 million infections and over 99,000 associated deaths each year in American hospitals.

Upon our arrival at UAB Hospital, Mike was rushed to the Intensive Care Unit. There were several doctors who cared for him; however, in a large teaching hospital one never knows who is in charge. They knew Mike was in trouble, and quickly began treatment with high-powered medicine. After several days without improvement, they tried the newest more powerful experimental medicines with no success. We stayed with him around the clock, seven days a week, waiting and sleeping in the waiting room. Later, after several days, we were able to get a room inside the hospital for out-of-town people to use. We took turns using the room for sleeping and taking showers.

I know it may seem that we were hovering over him, and may

have been over-reacting to the situation regarding a 42-year old adult. But who would be with him and care for him other than Barbara and me, along with his beloved sister Julie, his brother Roger, and Barbara's sister Carolyn. His grown children were not available to stay with him, and his ex-wife had no responsibility to stay. It didn't matter what age he was, he was our son whom we loved, and would have gladly taken his place in the hospital bed. But that was impossible, so all we could do was pray for him, be with him, talk to him, let him know that we were there, and that we loved him.

Week after week passed without any improvement in his condition. He developed sepsis, which is a condition where the body is fighting a severe infection that has spread through the bloodstream.

The doctors placed him in an induced coma, which is done often with seriously ill patients using a ventilator or breathing tube. They say that this helps the patients to heal better. It may do that, but I am convinced that this technique is used more for the medical personnel than for the patient. They cannot talk, move or anything, but I believe they can hear. Can you imagine lying there in that paralyzed condition, hearing the doctors and nurses and family members talking about you? Who knows what they hear. They could hear the doctors saying, "He's not going to live." I believe the induced coma is overused in hospitals, and should only be done as a very last resort.

I think about our son Roger years ago as he squeezed my finger to respond to my talking to him. That meant everything to us. If Mike could have responded to us in any way it would have made the situation much easier. I shudder to think of the living Hell he must have gone through.

Later, his organs began shutting down. His kidneys and liver finally stopped functioning and he was placed on a dialysis machine. After seven weeks at UAB, Mike passed away. We were all with him, Barbara and me, Julie and Philip, and Roger and Devona. Ralph and Janelle and Wayne and Sharon, our friends from home, were in the waiting room downstairs. In the final seconds of his life, Barbara and I were leaning over on him, holding him close to us, when he took two deep breaths and died. His eyes remained open, so I closed them with my fingers. To say the least, we were devastated. It was 4:30 p.m. on Friday, July 2nd, 2002. I said to Barbara, "I sure wish we could see the angels." The Bible says that angels will come and take us when we die, and I'm sure they came but we could not see them. My friend, Wayne Green, drove Barbara and me home later that night as the other family members followed us.

I have been to church and read the Bible a lot, but I continue to not understand the mysteries of death and the after-life. We all have heard great preachers give sermons, and read commentaries of the Bible by learned people. However, it is still not completely clear to me. After thinking about it, I realize why God didn't reveal everything there is to know about these matters. We are human beings. The wisdom of God is so powerful and far beyond our thinking, we can't understand it. I believe what we are told in the Bible is all He wanted us to know. Why would He give us every detail about death and Heaven before we die to experience it? He tells us that He has prepared for us a place that we are unable to imagine. God deals with us through faith, and we must have faith in Him to provide all these things that we do not know or understand in this life.

Mike's funeral was held at the Tuscumbia Church of Christ on July 5th, 2002. The church was filled with family and friends from home and from Montgomery. Several of my Senate colleagues and staff people were there, along with Governor Don Siegelman and other elected officials. He was buried at the Tuscumbia Oakwood Cemetery in a plot next to where his grandmother Jeffreys would be buried a few years later.

No one can ever understand what it is like to lose a child without experiencing it. The sadness and despair gradually gets better, but the loss can never completely leave our mind. We have done our best to cope with Mike's death and not feel sorry for ourselves. We find now after several years it is comforting to talk about him and the good memories we have of him. If you have lost a child and someone says to you, "I understand," ask them when they lost their child. If they have not lost a child, they have no idea what it's like, and they don't understand. I sometimes think to myself as I go about dealing with issues and problems, what Mike would recommend. We miss him every day of our lives, and try to keep in mind that he now knows where Heaven is and he would not want to come back.

CHAPTER SIXTEEN

I was re-elected to my sixth term as State Senator in November of 2002, and at that time had served 24 years. Pursuant to the rules adopted by the senate that year, I was named Dean of the Senate. The title really didn't mean much other than the honor of the position. I would be third in line to be presiding officer and was part of the top leadership. One of the best perks of the position was a new office at the front of the hall near the senate chamber. I had walked the long hall almost to the end since 1986 when we moved from the old Capitol Building into the renovated State Highway Department building across the street, which was later named The Alabama State House.

When we were at the Capitol, only a few senators had an office. Most of us had only a desk somewhere in a committee room. However, in my second term, I became a committee chairman and was given an office on the third floor to share with another senator. The office was only large enough for the two desks and a chair for each of us. The Capitol Building was literally about to fall in on us due to the lack of maintenance and repairs over the years. It had seen a hundred years of changes in the function of state government, and was no longer able to provide the necessary space and convenience required for today's Capitol Building. The Legislature had operated in the Alabama State House Building on Union Street at that time for 23 years. It seems like only yesterday when we moved and all the senators got a private office. It was so much better than before, especially when we had visitors from our districts come to Montgomery to see us. Although the offices now are very small, they give us a private place to talk with people and use the telephone.

There have been discussions about building a new State Legislative Building to meet the needs of expanding government, but I think if that happens it will probably be several years away. The present building needs repairs; the roof has always leaked and the wear and tear of thousands of people working and visiting has taken its toll. It's not a popular thing with the public to discuss more buildings, and spending government money on the operation of government. However, some day a governor and Legislature will have to face this issue. Over the years we learned to (as the saying goes) make do with what we have. I know most voters don't believe this, but I can assure them that the State of Alabama funds its state agencies less than any other state per capita, and we have the lowest tax burden than any other state. This would not be true if the State Legislature was not conservative.

These days the word conservative can mean several different things, but I am speaking about taxing, spending, saving, and borrowing money. One of the greatest things we do here in our state is we cannot spend more money than we take in. Most other states could use our approach in that regard. Should funding appropriations for the adopted state budget be more than the actual tax revenues received, then the governor must order pro-ration of the budget for that amount.

For example, if the budget appropriates $100 to a state agency, and the income for that year is 10 percent less, then the agency funds are reduced by 10 percent to $90 through the ensuing months of that fiscal year. Under the Federal government system if the funds do not meet the expenditures, the difference is added to what we know as the Federal Debt. I am aware that most of the examples and descriptions I use are very elementary to the people who deal with these matters of government, but I can only relate in terms that are understandable to me. That's one of the big problems in government, medical care, financial markets and other things today. It's all in the fine print, and none of us read it or understand it.

My work at Northwest Shoals Community College had been going well for several years. The Foundation was successful in raising funds to provide scholarships for students. The community of Northwest Alabama had accepted the college and much good was being done. After the merger of the campus on Highway 72 in Tuscumbia with the Technical School campus in Muscle Shoals, the Shoals campus had no gymnasium to play basketball and other indoor sports. The college needed a nice gymnasium for these activities, as well as a place for graduations and other large events.

Through the leadership of then president of the college, Dr. Larry McCoy, and the help of one of our Foundation Board members, Perry Bigbee, a new modern gym was constructed. Perry Bigbee and his family founded Bigbee Steel Buildings of Muscle Shoals and with their help we were able to build a building worth more than a million dollars for a few hundred thousand dollars. I remember my dear friend and former president of the Foundation, Bob Downie, signing the note with me at First Metro Bank. I wondered what would happen should the Foundation not be able to repay this loan. Bob Downie passed away in 2006 and the Shoals community suffered a great loss.

I loved my job at the college and all the people that I worked with, but after serving in the Senate and carrying out my duties for the College and Foundation for all those years, I began to consider retirement. When I became 65 years old, I had been employed at the college for 19 years. I had begun saving a little money over the last several years in an account which I called my Nursing Home Account; so, I did the math and Barbara and I decided it may be time for me to take another big step in our lives and leave a good job again.

So, I retired from Northwest Shoals Community College in 2003 and this time I believe the decision was a good one. It's nice not having to be at the office at 7:30 each morning to deal with all the events of the day. The only thing that I truly miss is the people that worked with me. The big college family was important to me.

They were all my friends, and continue to be today. During the last few years I have adjusted to the new lifestyle. We are very blessed and happy.

After our son Mike's death, I began looking into the problem of staph infections. Right away I learned that there are thousands of cases each year all over the country and many right here at home. I began to ask questions about how one would know if they are in a safe environment in the hospitals and medical facilities. I learned that there are no official records or reporting system in place for these facilities to allow the public to know which has a good or bad record with the contraction of infections. The State of Alabama does not have a law requiring hospitals to keep records and report infections. I have also learned there are over 25 other states that have laws regarding this, but they really don't do anything of substance to help the situation. I have read them all, and I have written a Bill to change the way this matter is handled in Alabama. The new law is named "The Mike Denton Infection Reporting Act."

I worked with the Alabama Hospital Association diligently to develop this legislation, which will make a difference in this life or death matter. My bargaining tool was that I had lost a son and thousands of others around the country lose loved ones every year. This is an issue that the public can relate to. The Federal government should have already passed legislation to require every hospital and medical facility to operate under the same procedures, but I'm sure the Congress would face even more opposition than I have trying to get the state law passed.

Without a law, the hospitals are dealing with public rumors regarding staph infections. When a patient is infected, they tell everyone what hospital they were in and the public seeks other places to have treatment. This is not good because a lot of people are convinced that the small local hospitals are the only hospitals that have a problem. That's not true; the big hospitals also have many cases.

If one would just consider how we regulate our other public establishments it becomes easier to understand why we need a law to deal with infections. Every restaurant, convenience store, and even beauty and barber shops have health ratings posted on the wall for public view. This is the law for them, and just about everyone is proud we have that law. The fastest way for one of these places to go out of business is to have a low score reported on the 6:00 o'clock news.

The hard fought process of passing legislation is very frustrating. At times we feel like it may not be worth the effort because most of the people don't know what is involved, and some of them don't even care. But I have always believed that leaders should try their best to do what they can do for the overall good of the public we serve.

CHAPTER SEVENTEEN

From His creation of the world, God implemented His concept of law in the earliest existence of everything and, applied reasonable order to exist among everything. Even birds, animals and fish have His order as part of their existence. It is easy to see this order and compliance when we see a great number of birds feeding on the ground. We can see them as they are all going about their business finding food as they walk around in all directions. However, make a loud noise and you will see them instantly fly away, and every one of them flying in the same direction. The same is true with large schools of fish when they move about in water. Can we imagine what it would be like if they all flew off in different directions? When we see a herd of cows walking back to the barn from the pasture, they are all walking in a line, one behind the other. Flocks of geese fly long distances in a V formation for reduced air resistance as they are flying.

God's instruction to Adam and Eve was one of the first examples of law and order given to His newly created humankind. In addition, we know very well what the punishment was after they disobeyed His orders in the Garden of Eden. His punishment was sure and quick. Later, while their sons Cain and Abel were working in a field they became involved in a conflict among themselves. Cain committed the sin of murder and killed his brother Abel.

God ordains all government. God endorses even the governments of the world who are not a free democracy. However, He may not approve of all their laws, but He does approve an organized structure of law and order to have a civil society. The Roman law of its time was very strict. It imposed harsh and swift punishment to those who dared to break the Laws. For instance, the two men crucified with Jesus were only robbers, yet they received the sentence of death.

Most countries of the world today would not impose the death penalty for the crime of robbery. Nevertheless, the robbers were executed with Jesus. However, Jesus was condemned to death for a so-called crime against Roman law by saying that He was the Son of God. After a night of ridicule and being beaten, He was sentenced to die with the cry of the large crowd insisting that they crucify Him. They made Jesus carry a cross through the city to the hill just outside the city. On the way there, Jesus became physically unable to carry it and a bystander was ordered to carry it for him. The hill known as Calvary was also referred to as, "The place of the skull." That was the place where all executions took place and the bodies of the victims were disposed of. However, the body of Jesus was allowed to be placed nearby in a new tomb owned by a secret follower.

While the Lord Jesus was on earth, He never became involved in the Law of the land. He neither condemned nor condoned slavery but He did speak of how slaves and their masters should conduct themselves. God never intended to create governments on the earth for the rule of humanity. I believe that God wants us to have order in all things and never condones crimes among people within any type of government established by man. Jesus was very clear about obeying the Laws of government. When some men were trying to trick Him said, "Tell us if it is right for us to pay taxes to Caesar or not?" Jesus responded to the person asking Him the question…"Whose image and name is on the coin?" The man answered, "Caesar's." Then Jesus said to the man, "Give to Caesar the things that are Caesar's, and give to God the things that are God's." (Matthew 22:21)

God, our Heavenly Father has His Laws in place for our spiritual life and does not make laws for man's civil governments. The laws made by man deal with thousands of issues concerning people at the local, state, and national level and they differ according to the government that imposes them. However, I am sure that God is disappointed and opposed to many of the laws that governments have in place which are very contrary to His will. However, we all are aware that God created us with a free will to obey or disobey.

After many years working with and in government, I came to the conclusion years ago that a Free Democratic System of government is a hard government to run. However, it is the very best type of government that has ever been. America's Representative form of government allows the people that it serves to have the power to have free elections to select the people whom they think will best represent their beliefs and values. With a Constitution and Bill of Rights, Americans have far more freedoms than most other countries of the world. Even with all the safeguards of our freedom, we have seen many changes over the short life of this great nation that we never thought we would ever see. Society is ever changing and with that, change brings demands from the people for government to change. They want new laws to deal with old ideas that are not acceptable anymore.

One would think that after all these years of being the most successful society the world has ever seen, we should have government oversight and regulations sufficient to live comfortably and safely within the Laws that we already have on the books at the present time. For example, the State of Alabama, which is relatively small, compared to many other states in our country has, as of today, about nine hundred amendments to its constitution, which was originally adopted in 1901.

This number of amendments to the constitution is not a problem in most other states. In 1901, large landowners wanted all governing power in the State to be under the control of the Legislature, which would be much easier to influence than the sixty-seven counties and dozens of cities and towns throughout the state. Thus allowing little or no power to the counties and cities to impose most laws or levy taxes without the approval of the Legislature. Property tax changes require a vote of the people. The State Legislature is in session 105 days each year. Its primary function is to pass the State Budget and make appropriations to the agencies of the State. However, most of the time is spent dealing with passing new laws or amending old laws. It is not unusual for the legislature to spend all its allotted time in session and never pass the State budget, requiring a special session for the adoption of a budget.

This has happened numerous times in the past and is a very costly and unnecessary lack of responsible action by elected officials. The Alabama State Legislature is set up to function much like the U.S. Congress in Washington. Personally, I think that they both could use some reform in the way they operate and do the people's business.

I have witnessed tremendous change in the way the system has operated over the last thirty-five years. We hear a lot of talk about special interest groups and their influence in our government. They are many, and they do have great influence regarding every issue that comes before the members for consideration. Forty years ago, I can only remember about six or eight lobbyists who represented special interest groups. Today, there are over six hundred registered lobbyists at the Alabama Legislature and thousands at the federal level of our government.

It is not a bad thing to have someone present in the process who can keep their clients informed and to express their views to the elected officials. The problem is the pressure overwhelms some elected officials with only one side of the issue and they do not always vote the issues in the best interest of the people who elected them.

In my opinion, The Golden Rule of elected office is "know the facts, keep your word, and do what YOU think is right." It is also my opinion that the political parties are out of control. We the people should elect people, not a party, and the elected individuals should think for themselves, not the party.

Throughout the history of the Earth, Law and Order has been in place for nature, animals, fish, and humans. All of which are the creations of God. Without this law and order, there would be complete chaos. All people have talents and abilities that others may not have. God through the help of the Holy Spirit gives the gifts He wishes for us to have according to His will and   a plan for our lives.

However, for one to have a plan, he or she must accept it from God and be willing to carry it out with the help of the Holy Spirit, which dwells within us. The Holy Spirit is our blessed helper and sustainer of all gifts. He helps us with these gifts and makes intercession for us unto God. We all have different gifts and if we carry them out, as God wants us to, they will help to encourage others to do the will of God with the plan given to them. These gifts are further explained in 1 Corinthians 12:1-11. We have so many wonderful gifts and we should try hard to appreciate them more as we go through life. I believe it is only natural that as we become older, we begin to appreciate them more and more.

The great apostle Paul gives us the inspired words of God regarding gifts in 1 Corinthians 13:1-13. (NCV) He said, "The greatest gift of all is LOVE."

These verses say, "I may speak in different languages of men or even angels. However, if I do not have love, then I am only a noisy bell or a ringing cymbal. I may have the gift of prophecy; I may understand all the secret things of God and all knowledge; and I may have faith so great that I can move mountains. But even with all these things, if I do not have love, then I am nothing. I may give everything I have to feed the poor.

And I may give my body as an offering to be burned. But I gain nothing by doing these things if I do not have love. Love is patient and kind. Love is not jealous, it does not brag, and it is not proud. Love is not rude, it is not selfish, and does not become angry easily. Love does not remember wrongs done against it. Love is not happy with evil, but is happy with the truth. Love patiently accepts all things. It always trusts, always hopes, and always continues strong. Love never ends."

We talked earlier about Law and how God gave us the freedom to obey or disobey His laws. Sadly, the majority of people choose not to obey them and continue living in sin. This is much more disappointing when we see people whom we know have heard the Gospel taught again and again but refuse to obey the Gospel of Christ and receive His Salvation. It is heart breaking to know these situations are occurring all around us every day.

The choices to accept or reject the gifts given to us by God and will only last while we continue to be alive here on earth. At death, His offer ends. We will be, according to His judgment, saved or lost for eternity.

The spiritual laws given to us in the Bible are the Laws of God and cannot be changed as civil laws are amended because society disagrees with them. God's Laws are the same yesterday, today, and tomorrow. As taught in the scriptures, Jesus did not take a position regarding civil laws enacted by the government. He advocated obeying them although He may not agree with them. His mission on earth was to go about His Fathers business teaching forgiveness from sin.

The world had waited thousands of years for the savior to come as was taught in the Old Testament. However, not all believed at that time.

When we have God's Laws and the civil laws of government to live by, a great number of people will disagree with the way we should live our lives. First, God's Law is the Supreme Law. Man's law cannot overrule it so, if we are obedient to God's laws, we will have very little trouble obeying the laws of man. Using just a few examples, we can see that at times the laws of man are in direct conflict with God's Laws.

Those of us who have lived into our senior years have witnessed some of these conflicts. With the fast changing social changes in recent years, civil law is conflicting with God's Law. One is the issue of the practice of homosexuality, which is sin and against God's Law.

We are experiencing an avalanche of public acceptance condoning this sin through every public medium and it is becoming worse every day. These issues along with making same-sex marriage lawful are both condemned very clearly in the Bible.

In 1 Corinthians 6: 9-11, Paul was addressing the troubled Church at Corinth. "Surely you know that the people who do wrong will not inherit God's kingdom. Do not be fooled. Those who sin sexually, worship idols, take part in adultery, those who are male prostitutes, or men who have sexual relations with other men, those who steal, are greedy, get drunk, lie about others, or rob…these people will not inherit God's kingdom. In the past, some of you were like that, but were washed clean. You were made holy, and you were made right with God in the name of the Lord Jesus Christ and in the Spirit of our God." There is forgiveness if we accept it.

The issue of women having sex with women has become just as prevalent today in our society. The Bible teaches us that sin is sin. However, homosexuality is one of the hardest for me to understand. I have always been amazed that humans would ever do such an act. Growing up, we young people became aware that something was wrong when we rarely saw a woman dressed like a man or a man who expressed female characteristics. Of course, that has even changed in this day and time, one cannot always tell by looking and talking to a person if they are Gay or not. Some say that people are born this way but I do not know how or why this happens.

God is our judge and He will decide these matters when the time of judgment comes. It is interesting that the Bible says, "The practice of it is a sin." It does not address the fact of having or not having the condition of being homosexual. It says, "Those who take part in sexual sins, who have sexual relations with people of the same sex." (1 Timothy 1:10)

CHAPTER EIGHTEEN

Lawful abortion is another sinful law of man's government that has become commonplace in today's society. God said in the Bible, Jeremiah 1: 5 (NCV) "Before I made you in your mother's womb, I chose you. Before you were born, I set you apart for a special work. I appointed you as a Prophet to the nations."

It is interesting how we may look at the sins mentioned in the Bible. We are quick to think that one sin may not be as bad as another sin may be.

As is said in 1 Corinthians 6:10-11, can we choose which sin is very bad or one that is not so bad? The scripture does not read that way. Suppose a person was a robber and he condemned another who is guilty of adultery. Is he a better person in the law of God? If the murderer condemns the one who tells lies, is he any better? Therefore, we should be careful when we condemn others for their sins. Remember what Matthew 7:5 said? "You hypocrite! First take the log out of your own eye. Then you will see clearly to take the speck out of your friend's eye."

If someone asks me, "What do you think is the most despicable sin one could ever commit?" I suppose I would say, "The child molester is the worst." To me it is the most deplorable sin to harm a Child, especially sexually. Yet, God is the Judge. However, I just have a feeling that He may agree with me. Jesus loved little children so much while He was on earth.

It seems that with more technology coming into being, the need for spiritual values are becoming less. The internet and social media has exploded and is projecting a negative effect to the values of the teachings of God. The younger generation is the greatest part of society affected by this rush of acceptance of ungodly activities. There are several reasons for this.

Young people have lived during a more liberal time regarding spiritual rules and laws. Parents of past years have become less restrictive and more accepting of social change brought about through technology. The younger people have access to a completely different world than did we parents of yesterday. There is hardly a TV program on the air today that does not allude to sex, crime, drugs, foul language, alcohol, and homosexuality to the point of expecting the viewer to accept them. When this continues to go on, people begin to think that it is an acceptable thing.

Where is this all leading our world? Who will stand up and say "enough…stop it now!" Is this not something that Christians should demand of government?

The insulting and distasteful things that are on TV are very bad but I understand that the internet is filled with hard-core pornographic material, which is even worse. The internet is open and available to anyone twenty-four hours a day, seven days a week and is free to be seen by children as well as adults. I understand that experts have determined that pornography is addictive. It will cause one to suffer from the sin of lust, and may cause sexual crimes. I think looking at pictures or movies with a lustful eye is just as sinful as seeing these things in person.

God's law is extremely strict regarding this sin. In reading (John 8:3-11) a woman was caught in the act of adultery. The teachers of the law and the Pharisees brought the woman who had been caught in the act of adultery to Jesus. They forced her to stand before the people. They said to Jesus, "Teacher, this woman was caught having sexual relations with a man who is not her husband. The Law of Moses commands that we stone to death every woman who does this. What do you say we should do?" They were asking this to trick Jesus so they could have some charge against him. Then Jesus bent over and started writing on the ground with his finger. When they continued to ask Jesus their question, he rose up and said. "Anyone here who has not sinned can throw the first stone at her."

Then Jesus bent over again and wrote on the ground. Those who heard Jesus say that began to walk away one by one, first the older men and then the others. Jesus was left alone with the woman standing before him. Jesus rose up again and asked her, "Woman, where are they? Has no one judged you guilty?" She answered, "No one, sir." Then Jesus said, "I also don't judge you guilty. You may go now, but don't sin anymore." The old Law of Moses was strict but the New Law given by Jesus is much stricter in this subject. Matthew 5:28 (NCV) addresses such a sin saying, "But I tell you that if anyone looks at a woman and wants to sin sexually with her, in his mind he has already done that sin with the woman."

The sin of adultery has always been a problem for people since we have been on the earth. It is not fair to place all the blame of sexual sins on the young people of today. Movies, TV, The Internet, and Printed Materials are the culprit. The problem is adults have allowed this situation to perpetuate into a monster sin in our generation that is responsible for crime, death and the loss of souls. To stop the message, we must stop the sender of the message with strong laws. With all the problems of the world, this issue is one of the greatest threats our country is facing. It is very sad that our elected government officials and church leaders never think about this problem or try to do anything about it. It is a shame!

With the thousands of laws passed by the Federal and State governments in the country, one should think that the citizens would be safe, happy and healthy. However, it seems that making more laws by man is not the answer to the problem of crime. The crime rate continues to go up every year and it seems to be an unstoppable monster. One that is destroying the greatest civilization the world has ever known.

In recent years, drugs have become the major cause of crime at all levels of age and social groups. The more expensive drugs appeal to the higher income levels of people and the prescription drugs are popular with the middle incomes who buy them from robbers or dishonest drugs dispensing people. Then, there are the low-income people who make their own drugs using over the counter mixtures of a deadly potion called "meth" which is a sure killer.

Therefore, with the self-perpetuating elements of guns, drugs, alcohol, sex, and sin, our destiny is quickly becoming a country of lawless anarchy while overflowing with laws. It is evident that fixing the laws is not the solution to our problems. We must work harder to fix the heart and soul of man.

Not all laws composed by man are good for us and benefit our wellbeing. Some of them make us do things contrary to Gods Laws. The average person who does not know the difference will follow the laws of man down the path of destruction. It would be wonderful if all our laws included a section similar to the code of ethics for Medical Doctors, written with explicit detail. I have read the American Medical Association's code of ethics and I am encouraged with its sincerity for the welfare of the patient. It is saying in short… "DO NO HARM."

Throughout the ages, God has given numerous Laws for man to follow. We are more familiar with some such as the rules set out to Adam and Eve and the Ten Commandments. However, God knew He must do away with some of the old laws and give a new law that applied to all people never to be changed. God knew the only way to do this was to give His Son as a sacrifice for the sins of the world. God did this and His Son Jesus the Christ taught the New Law to the people with the help of His chosen twelve men. They were just common people, which He selected to help Him as disciples.

As we read in the Gospels of the New Testament, Jesus did numerous miracles to prove He was the Son of God. According to Gods plan, it was necessary for Jesus to die and the Roman Government crucified him. As we think about laws and ponder just how many laws we live under today, one may think that there is a law dealing with just about everything. Well, I have good news for you! Galatians 5:22-23 says: "Love, Joy, Peace, Patience, Kindness, Goodness, Faithfulness, and Self-control. There is no law that says these things are wrong."

Several sins pointed out in The Holy Scriptures are misunderstood as to what the New Testament means. For example: The partaking of wine. We know that being drunk is sinful, but it refers to Elders and Deacons as "not taking much wine." Does this say the drinking of some wine is acceptable? In addition, women should not dress in men's clothing, and men should not dress in clothing of women and if a woman's head is to be covered.

There are dozens of issues that people have differences with regarding the Worship services. Some think that the seventh day of the week is the day of worship. When it is clear that Christ said, The Church should come together and meet on the first day of the week. That is what the first century church did. "They came together on the first day of the week." It is amazing that many people continue to think the Sabbath Day is Sunday. "Remember the Sabbath and keep it Holy" is part of the Old Law.

Other issues regarding the worship service are, baptism, instrumental music, solo singing, women preaching or speaking in the worship, women teaching men, taking the Lords Supper, the modesty of clothing, the leadership of Elders and Deacons, giving to the Church, eating a meal in the church building, caring for orphan children, voting on Church issues and many others things.

I believe all Christians who are sincere believers that Christ is the Son of God want to do the right thing in worshiping Him. However, we all have a tendency to do the things the way our parents did as we grew up. The same is true regarding worshiping God. As we said before, it is very confusing as to who we believe when there are so many different churches and all of them doing things different. First, we were raised to respect our parents and trust their judgments in matters that we do not yet understand. And, that's good. However, as we become older and are able to read the Bible and understand for ourselves what it says, we are not morally obligated to believe and do as our parents did regarding spiritual matters, which we find are contrary to the teachings of the Bible.

This situation is hard for us to deal with. However, many

scriptures address this issue in the Bible and our soul is at stake. If we find that our beliefs differ from our parents, we should obey God. It is not that we should stop loving and caring for them just as much but, we are obligated to God in matters of our salvation. We are to study the scriptures and find Bible answers to questions we have as to what the truth is regarding our worship.

We only have one chance to be sure that we are pleasing God and that is while we are still alive here on earth. While there is still time, we must be very sure of our eternal destiny. The mystery of death has always been intriguing to me. It is very clear that we must all personally face this once in a lifetime event, which we have never experienced before.

We have information in the Bible about it but no one has ever died and returned to give us exact details about what happens. I have witnessed the death of others and felt so helpless to see them as they slipped away. From the scriptures, we know a few of the facts but we can only think in our mind what it will be exactly like. The Bible says that our mind cannot imagine what Death, Heaven or Hell will really be like. We cannot comprehend eternity. Never, ever ending time!

The Bible does tell us enough to have an idea about the choice we have for where we will spend our eternal life. We know at death, God's angels will take us to Heaven or the Devil's angels will take us to Hell. It will be too late to change our destiny then.

Most people have an understanding that Heaven is a wonderful place, even beyond our wildest imagination. However, we do not often talk or think about Hell. Some people do not believe that Hell is a real place. We can go to Heaven through the grace of the Lord Jesus Christ and it is so easy if we determine in our heart to follow His instructions.

We should be careful regarding the sins we have mentioned and remember that God will forgive us regardless of the sin committed if we choose to come back. Some may become so discouraged thinking they have gone too far into sin that they cannot get back to be saved. We have the assurance of Christ our Savior that we can...no matter what. He will take us back.

In addition to the sins mentioned before, there is the question of divorce, which is prevalent in our society. Remember the woman at the well drawing water? Jesus came by and talked with her. She had five previous husbands and was living with another man at the time. One would think that this woman had gone too far to get back to God. Nevertheless, read John 4:7-19. Jesus offered her the "living water" of forgiveness.

He did not condone her situation but I believe He forgave her. She asked for the living water then went back into town praising Him and telling all the people what He had said to her.

The decision we have to make now before we die is… where do we want to spend eternity after death? Death is surely coming to all of us and it is no respecter of age. God has given us the choice of using our own freewill regarding this very important matter. He loves us beyond our imagination, and wants us to come to Heaven. However, without our acceptance of His plan for eternal life through Christ Jesus, we will be condemned to Hell.

WHAT WE MUST DO TO BE SAVED

We must **hear**, read, or be taught the plan of salvation given by Jesus Christ.

We must **believe** with all our heart that Jesus is the Son of God.

We must **confess** our sins, admitting that we are a sinner.

We must **repent** of our sins by turning away from them.

We must **be baptized**. Buried in water for the forgiveness of sin.

We must **remain faithful** living the life of a Christian until death.

Would we really want to take that chance?

CHAPTER NINETEEN

Barbara's mother, whom we all called Mamaw, had developed congestive heart failure several years ago and the doctor said she may not survive the condition for more than a year or two. However, she managed to live with it for more than 10 years. When she had serious problems she was sent to the hospital, and through medication, the fluid around her heart was reduced. She went through several of these bouts over the years. Also, when Mamaw developed a major blockage of her intestines, this required a very serious operation. At her age we were worried about her. The surgeon removed the affected area and installed a colostomy. This was a terrible experience for her and the family. She was very self-conscious as anyone would be, and needed help with it each day. She lived in an apartment in Tuscumbia, alone at the time, so one of the daughters, Barbara or Carolyn, or the family angel Julie, would come to her apartment to help her with the colostomy. After the surgery, her first question to a doctor was, "Is it possible to have this procedure reversed?" The doctor said it could be after about a year if she did well otherwise, but it would be a very serious operation.

As the months went by she would remind the doctor that she wanted the reversal done as soon as possible. So, in six months, she checked into the hospital to have the surgery. It was very hard on her and she had a few close calls, but she pulled out and went home happy. After going home we all kept close watch on her. One of the girls stayed with her overnight most of the time. We also arranged for her to have an emergency call device she could wear as a necklace, but she never wanted to use it. Later, as she healed, we got a lady to come and live with her around the clock.

It seems these days we live in now are so different than when my grandparents were old and stayed with members of the family. Now everyone has a job, and there is always a reason we cannot keep our loved ones in our homes anymore. This has created a very large industry in our society called assisted living. If one does not qualify for Medicaid, he or she cannot be accepted in a nursing home or assisted living without the extremely high price of private pay. Alabama has the poorest Medicaid funding program in the nation. Mamaw did not qualify for Medicaid because her social security check of just over $600 per month was too much. So that meant the family was responsible for all her medicine and the medical costs not covered by Medicare, which covers most of the hospital and doctor charges for people over 65. For one to be denied Medicaid, who only receives just over $600 a month, is absolutely ridiculous.

We could see she was not completely happy staying at home with the lady living with her. She needed a better situation. We researched all the assisted living facilities around the area and found the perfect one for her. Wellington Place was a new facility that was located within a mile from our home. The people were very nice and cared for her like she was their own mother. It was very clean and the food was excellent. They offered all kinds of programs for the residents, including exercise, games, live entertainment, and church services. She was happy in her new private room with all her cherished things from home.

I loved Mamaw like she was my own mother; after all I had known her much longer than I did my own sweet mother, who gave birth to me and cared for me in ways that I will never know. God bless her sweet soul. Barbara's mother was happy at Wellington Place and we never regretted a penny of the money it cost for her to live there. Barbara and her sister Carolyn shared the cost beyond her little monthly social security check to pay Wellington

Place. We all provided any other needs that she had.

Each week when the senate was in session and Barbara and I went to Montgomery, Mamaw always worried about our traveling on the highway. I can hear her now saying, "Y'all be careful." Julie and Carolyn visited her every day, and the phone calls from all of us were numerous. She had a few episodes related to the congestive heart condition from time to time, which seemed to take a further toll on her after each one.

Mama's cardiologist was a woman doctor whom she trusted totally. If the doctor told her anything, that's what Mamaw wanted to do. The doctor also loved her and always treated her with high respect and kindness. We felt the time may be drawing near that Mamaw could leave us, but she did not want us to know it.

Over the years she had been like my parents regarding uttering the words "I love you." She just didn't ever say it; however, she began to change during the last several years and said it often. We always said it to her. I cannot remember a time after a visit with her, or at the end of a telephone talk, that she didn't end the conversation with "I love you." I think her saying these words to all of us over the years had a powerful influence on us. We all use this affectionate salutation now as we communicate with family members, and even others whom we feel fondly toward.

The term "I love you" will melt a heart of steel and can change a person's life. It also is very contagious to others. I have used the words in ending a phone conversation with people I like and think the world of, but some of them just can't say "I love you too." With some, the best you can ever get back from them is "You too." When I say this to my brother he will always say, "OK." Some men may think it's sissy to say such a thing to another man, although they know he really loves him. We all love people without being in love with them. I love my neighbors, but I'm not in love with them. "I love you" are the sweetest words one can ever say to another person. Of course, we should never go around using the words loosely or flippantly, but I can assure you that using these words to the right people, at the right time, will help you and them.

When we realized the time had come for Mamaw to take her Heavenly flight, we were all in her room as she slowly drifted away in death. She had not spoken a word for hours, however, after she took a shallow breath she raised her hand and clearly said, "save me." I again thought about the angels that were there and could not be seen. It was March 12, 2008, at 6:30 p.m.

The staff at Wellington Place had prepared food and coffee for the family while we waited with her. Barbara, Carolyn and Julie read several scriptures to her during her last hours and took turns lying beside her on the bed. Mamaw was 86 years old and always looked so pretty, with her nails polished and her hair styled nicely. The funeral was beautiful. It was conducted in a manner she would have wanted. A long-time friend of the Jeffreys family, James Alan Horton, gave the brief message along with the playing of two songs from one of my gospel albums.

She was laid to rest at the Tuscumbia Oakwood Cemetery beside her husband Eugene, and next to her beloved grandson Mike. Again, love lifted us out of the valley of death and sorrow. Through faith we are assured we shall see our loved ones again some day. That love also allows us to recall the fond memories of them, and through our faith we realize that some day we will take this journey into eternity ourselves. While we are alive here on earth, we have the choice, through faith, as to where we will spend eternity.

CHAPTER TWENTY

I began developing back trouble in the early '80s and tried almost everything to alleviate the pain. For a long time, my best results came through my long-time chiropractor friend, Jerry Plexco. He helped me a lot and kept me going for years.

Later, the pain moved to my right leg and became increasingly worse. I sought the advice of another friend and pharmacist regarding a doctor who did treatment for this symptom. He recommended that I call a local orthopedic doctor. After being examined by him, he suggested surgery for a severe disc problem in my lower back. Most people refer to this condition as a ruptured disc. I could hardly walk, and the pain was horrific. The doctor did surgery on my back and was assisted by my old friend and general surgeon Dr. John Mims, who was our family doctor.

After the surgery was over, the recovery was very slow and I was disappointed because I did not feel my back was completely well. At this time I was working at the bank and they were very considerate by allowing me the time off needed for recovery. I also missed several budget meetings in Montgomery as a member of the Senate Finance Committee.

In the ensuing years after changing jobs to work for the Community College, I underwent additional lower back surgery and a disc fusion surgery in my neck. These surgeries were done by a very popular neurosurgeon in Birmingham. My recovery this time was considerably faster. The doctor and I became friends, and I suppose one could say I have been one of his best customers for over 20 years. After fully recovering from the surgeries from time to time, I continued to see my chiropractor when my back seemed to become a problem again.

Several years later, I began having a problem that seemed very diffrent than the past experiences. Although my lower back was uncomfortable, the pain was never down my leg as before. I had for a long time experienced ear problems also, and some unsteadiness, but the doctors could not find anything wrong with my back other than a small condition of spinal stenosis, which is a narrowing of the spinal column pressing on the nerves.

I had the opinion of a spinal specialist in Birmingham and other doctors. The ear problem was never diagnosed, and three ear doctors could not explain the problem. They tried every known medicine to correct the feeling in the ears, with no success. Over a period of several years I learned to deal with this condition, and now I know what the ear problem was.

As time passed, my lower back continued to be a problem, and my legs just didn't work as they should. There was not a lot of pain; I just could not walk well. It seemed as if I was trying to walk with a shuffle, like Tim Conway who played on the Carol Burnett TV program years ago. My family doctor recommended I be checked by a neurologist and referred me to one. This doctor told me that I did not have Parkinson's disease or any neurological problem. His simple test showed I was normal, but I continued to become worse. I was referred to a therapy center in Muscle Shoals to see if they could help me walk and control my balance better. I tried hard to allow the therapy to help, but it didn't.

The next legislative session was bad for me. I could hardly walk from my office to the Senate Chamber. Finally, I resorted to using a cane. It made me feel old and depressed. On several occasions while I was in Montgomery, I went to a chiropractor and received some temporary relief.

At the end of the legislative session I called my friend the neurosurgeon in Birmingham, for an appointment. He reviewed my x-rays. After finding an extreme separation of my abdominal muscles, called Separated Rectus, he referred me to another surgeon in Birmingham to repair it before proceeding further with my back. The other doctor checked me and said there was no way he would operate on me for this condition. Going back to the neurosurgeon, he agreed that I should have surgery for the spinal stenosis to trim the bone away from my spinal cord. I am told that doctors don't like to do this surgery unless there is no other choice.

In the meantime, my walking and balance were so bad I fell several times and could not function well at all. Surgery was scheduled at Brookwood Hospital in Birmingham. Barbara and Julie carried me to the hospital. I went through the maze of questions and information one has to endure when checking into a hospital.

The surgery was done and I was sent home in two days wearing a brace and feeling terrible. The next day was Saturday. I stayed in bed most of the time. That night the pain was so bad in my lower back it was hard to bear. I could not get relief from pain pills so Barbara asked our son and daughter-in-law, Roger and Devona, to come over to help us. I had tried to get from the bed to a chair and fell on the floor. I could not move my legs. Roger, Devona, and Barbara looked after me all night. The next morning, Sunday, Roger called the doctor in Birmingham, and luckily he called back very soon. He told them to get me to the hospital for an MRI.

They found a major blood clot on my spinal cord. I was paralyzed and could not move my legs and feet. The doctor instructed the hospital to airlift me to Brookwood in Birmingham soon. The Airvac crew delivered me. I was immediately taken into surgery. This was my second major surgery on my back in less than a week. Later, I remember the doctor coming into ICU and saying, "Bobby, move your toes." As I moved them he said, "Thank God."

The day after this surgery, the doctor came in my room and said, "We have to do another procedure on you, and this time it will be on your head." I could not believe it. I was so groggy from the two surgeries I really didn't understand what was going on and why. Later, he told me that he and his associates knew when I could not walk upright after the other procedures they needed to do a brain scan and investigate further into my problem. They prepared me for another, even more serious operation, the third one in a week. The doctors found out for sure what my problem was this time; it's called hydrocephalus.

Normal pressure hydrocephalus (NPH) is a neurological condition which usually affects people over 55 years old. It is an accumulation of cerebrospinal fluid causing the ventricles of the brain to enlarge, stretching the nerve tissue. One quarter million Americans with some of the same symptoms as Dementia, Alzheimer's, or Parkinson's, may actually have NPH as I did. I believe my older brother Johnny was a victim of misdiagnosis of this condition. He also was referred to a neurologist, and died sitting in his chair within a year of unknown causes.

It's often difficult to tell the difference between the symptoms, because the symptoms in many ways are similar. However, the feeling of feet glued to the floor, or difficulty walking, is the main difference. This fluid is necessary to cushion the delicate brain and spinal cord from injury. Normally, the bloodstream absorbs most of the fluid produced on a daily basis. Every day our body produces a certain amount. If that amount is excessive, then over time the brain will be affected causing the normal pressure hydrocephalus.

A surgery procedure has been developed over the last several years to allow doctors to implant a shunt between the skull and the skin, then make a small hole in the skull and insert a tube to pass through the brain and into the lateral ventricle. The tube coming from the other end of the shunt is directed through the fatty tissue of the body, just under the skin, passing down through the abdominal cavity where the excessive fluid is absorbed.

After this third surgery, I have never experienced anything like what I went through the next few days in the ICU. I cannot shake off the memories of those hours of my life. I suppose the brain surgery, after the two back surgeries, caused me more than the usual discomfort after serious surgery. As I drifted in and out of consciousness, it was hard to determine what was real or unreal from sounds and visions penetrating my mind. The effects of the back procedure had my complete lower body immobile, and the brain operation was overwhelming my entire being. I thought of my dear son Mike and what he went through for weeks before he died in a Birmingham hospital just a few years before. And I thought about our baby son Roger, as he lay with a critical injury to his brain. I began to be encouraged that I was not experiencing as much trauma as they had been through before me.

When the ICU experience was over, I found myself having to learn how to do things I had always taken for granted. My walking slowly came around to normal after starting out from a wheelchair, then to a walker, then to a cane, and later on my own.

When I left the hospital I was admitted for two weeks to Lakeshore Rehabilitation Hospital in Birmingham, and after being dismissed there, I underwent three weeks at Helen Keller Hospital Physical Therapy Center back home. I was doing well at first, but I was not where I should have been with my recovery. I later found my motor skills were getting worse, and my balance was not good. We began to think that surely I was not about to have a relapse of the hydrocephalus.

After calling for an appointment to see my doctor again, I returned to see him. I was sent to the hospital to check the shunt. His associate ran tests using dye in the tube and found that it was not draining. I was very disappointed.

When things like this occur, we can only do as the doctor recommends and have faith in them to do the right thing. I relied on my faith in God to do His will with me, and of course I prayed that His will would be for me to get better. Again, I could hardly believe I was going to have yet another surgery. By this time, I was told I was on the prayer lists of most churches around the area, and of my many friends in Montgomery. After this next surgery, I went through the same rehabilitation program again, but this time it was much easier than before.

My thoughts continue to remember the people at the hospital who were so nice to me. The nurses and the staff were special, but my memories are clearer of the faces of some of the people who were there like me, but would never be able to walk again. Some who had brain surgery and may never be who they were again.

Barbara stayed with me night and day, and helped me through it all. She has always been there for me, in sickness or in health, for better or for worse, for richer or for poorer. As we grow older and reflect back on our lives, it's exactly as Solomon in the Bible describes the things we have considered to be important. Things like making money, popularity, power, and tons of other things. He said at the end it's all vanity. Our relationship with God, our fellow man, and our family, are the real things we should be concerned about because all the other things will not matter.

Sadly, a year after my last surgery, Dr. Even Zieger, my friend and neurosurgeon, along with his wife, were both killed when he crashed his personal airplane.

CHAPTER TWENTY-ONE

After serving thirty-two years in the Alabama State Senate, I knew it was time to give the job to someone younger. I decided not to seek re-election in 2010. The two hundred mile trip every week was becoming difficult for me. Although I continued to do my job with vigor and dedication, I felt that it was not fair for me to continue to hold the office for another term. I truly loved doing the job. The greatest reward was being able to help people who did not know where to turn or what to do about a problem they had. As someone once said, "What do I do when I don't know what to do"?

I believe one of the saddest times of my life was when I walked out of the Senate Chamber for the last time and saying goodbye to friends that I had served with and, some of the Staff members I had worked with for the thirty-two years that I had been there. I knew that I would never see most of them ever again. Especially, Carolyn, my only personal staff member and loyal friend who had worked with me for thirty years. I will be forever thankful for her help as we served the people of my Northwest Alabama District and the State of Alabama.

The first two years after retiring was difficult for me to deal with. It seems that I could not relax because I thought I had somewhere to go or someone to call. For all those years, my time was totally consumed with doing my Senate job and my job at the College.

I suppose this experience can be described as the way we feel after the death of a friend or love one. It hurts so bad for a long time and then the feeling begins to subside according to the depth of the relationship. Some will come to our mind every day, and some occasionally. As the days and years go by, we only have the memories without the hurt. However, a few will be "forever friends" and will live in our heart until we die.

This same experience is true as I turned sixty-five years old and retired from Northwest –Shoals Community College in Muscle Shoals. However, this situation was somewhat different. I had been Director of Development at the College for eighteen years. I organized the College Foundation, a 501-3c Corporation to raise funds for scholarships and special needs projects for the college. My job was also responsible for administering the scholarships funded by the Foundation. The organization continues to make progress and is very helpful to students who need help attending college.

There was a great deal of difference in the retirement experiences because the College job was at home here in Muscle Shoals and the Senate job was at the Alabama State Capitol two hundred miles away. After retirement from the College, I have not been in contact with all of the Facility and Staff however, I do see some of them from time to time around the community or at College functions. I have been invited to speak and sing at some graduation events.

It did not take me long to start enjoying some of the life style of retirement. It is nice not to get out of bed and rush through the shower and shave, put on a suit and tie, grab some breakfast and be at work by seven thirty in the mornings. However, after a few months, I found myself so busy I do not know how I ever had time to work. The days are flying by so fast. Then, there is the factor of age. I soon began to feel older and found that I could not do things that have been normal all by life. I have found that I cannot do things that I want to do…and I do not want to do things that I can do. It is said that we are as old as we feel and I think that is true. At seventy-six,…some days I do feel old.

Because of the events over the years of my life, I am always mindful of the possibility of another accident or sickness attacking my family. When things have been going good for an extended time, I have the uneasy feeling that some tragedy may come upon us again.

I know it is a weakness of faith to feel that way but I cannot help it. I find myself continually thinking that something bad is going to happen. We have been blessed after my last surgeries in that our family has had a few years of wellbeing. And then the monster strikes again.

Last year, our Daughter Julie began having severe headaches that continued for several days. Her husband Philip took her to the ER at a local Hospital on a Sunday morning and they did a CT scan on her head.

The CT showed six large spots on her brain. One was the size of a walnut, and five the size of a grape. They admitted her and carried her to a room in the hospital to decide what to do. It was obvious that the situation was very serious and that time was critical. The ER doctor ordered pain medicine and two other Doctors came to the room to see her. An Oncologist and Internal Medicine Doctor. Why would she need an Oncologist when they did not know for sure without running test? They could only think "cancer" and did not know what to do. The only Neurosurgeon in the area left to go on vacation before taking a biopsy.

Julie was talking at that point but within a few hours, she became un-responsive. We were very worried. Shortly, a cardiologist friend of ours saw us standing in the hallway and ask why we were there. We told him about Julie and he went to the Nursing Station and pulled her file. The Doctor came back to Julie's room and said, to Philip, "You have to get her out of here now!" I handed him my cell phone with my Neurosurgeons' phone number in Birmingham. He called him and they made plans for her to fly to Birmingham as soon as possible. The Helicopter arrived and before they could leave, the Doctor in Birmingham called and said the Hospital there would not take her as an ER patient. Therefore, they took her to Huntsville Hospital. The Huntsville Hospital staff received her and quickly made arrangements for a team of Doctors to assess her condition which by then had become extremely critical. They conducted a test and ordered a new MRI of her brain.

The next day, a Neurosurgeon performed surgery at the location of the only accessible liaison at the side of her brain and removed it. As our family waited for the Doctor to come out of the operating room and tell us what he had found, we all prayed. I had already asked God repeatedly to "please do not let this thing… whatever it is, take another one of my children." When the door finally opened and the Doctor came out, we were in a state of shock. The Doctor said he had successfully removed the object and he could tell that it was not Cancer. Cancer would be a tumor and this was a mass substance of infection. He said he had never seen an infection this severe before. They began giving Julie massive doses of medication for infection.

However, they did not know exactly what type she needed until they found out what the infection was. The Infection Disease Specialist sent the removed object to Mayo Clinic for a very fast report of the infection so the correct treatment could be given for the remaining five masses in her brain.

Julie was in a coma and required to be on a ventilator. She was in very guarded condition in NICU while waiting for the result found by Mayo. We sat in the waiting room around the clock and went in to see her at the allowed times.

Two days past and Mayo reported that Julie had an almost unheard of infection called, Streptococcus Intermedius. Only a few cases of this deadly infection have been reported in the brain area. We were overjoyed when the

Infectious Disease Doctor told us that they had been giving Julie the exact type medicine that she needed while they waited for Mayo to report.

With the remaining five masses being inoperable, the only hope to stop the infections was to kill it with medication. Therefore, that is what they proceeded to do. Julie remained in the Hospital for two weeks, then moved to the Rehab Hospital for three weeks. She responded very well as she learned how to regain her motor skills. Within a month or two, Julie was her old self again.

It is strange to me that some people get older and continue to want more as they age. I have never understood that type of reasoning. Maybe I'm just wrong, but as I get older I want less. I have lived my life working hard for material things. If I had all the money back that I wasted on cars, trucks, camper trailers, and things in my life, I would have a lot of money. I like new cars and nice things, but somehow they just don't appeal to me as much as they once did. My wife and I are down to having only two cars now. One is twelve years old and the other one is four. Most of our travel is just a few places and they are all within two or three miles from home. They are church, the doctor, drug store, post office, Walmart, and a few restaurants.

I find myself not worrying about the fashion of my old suits in my closet. Being older takes away a lot of the pressures of what other people think about how we are dressed. I've never been old before, but I'm finding it has a lot of good parts, not counting the aches and pains in the body.

It is my prayer that all who read this book have love, peace, and happiness in your life, and that you will ask God for His guidance each day. Thank you God!